THE REASONABLENESS

OF THE

CHRISTIAN FAITH

BY

DAVID S. CAIRNS

PROFESSOR OF DOGMATICS AND APOLOGETICS
IN THE UNITED FREE CHURCH COLLEGE
ABERDEEN

HODDER AND STOUGHTON
LONDON   NEW YORK   TORONTO
MCMXVIII

<u>Printing Statement:</u>

Due to the very old age and scarcity of this book,
many of the pages may be hard to read due to the
blurring of the original text, possible missing pages,
missing text, dark backgrounds and other issues
beyond our control.

Because this is such an important and rare work, we
believe it is best to reproduce this book regardless of
its original condition.

Thank you for your understanding.

THE REASONABLENESS OF
THE CHRISTIAN FAITH

TO

MY SISTER

PREFACE

THE following volume is based on a short-hand report of four addresses delivered at the invitation of the Christian Evidence Society to undergraduates of Cambridge University and others in the Examination Hall in the spring of 1913. These addresses were re-delivered to soldier audiences in the base camps at Rouen and Havre and elsewhere in 1916, and the additional material, due to the restatement of the argument under war conditions, is incorporated in the Epilogue. It has been thought better to retain in the earlier chapters the freedom of an unwritten address, though at the cost of some obvious drawbacks. I am much indebted to many friends for their assistance in the production of these lectures, in particular to Dr. T. R. Glover, for an admirable summary published in the *Cambridge Magazine*; to Professor Oman of Westminster College,

Cambridge, for his invaluable help in Cambridge and in Rouen Camp; to Professor Burkitt and to Father Waggett of the Christian Evidence Society; to Mr. Joseph Callan and Mr. Arthur Reade of the Y.M.C.A. in Rouen and Havre; and to my brother, the Rev. W. T. Cairns, and Dr. Glover, for their revision of the proofs, and to all those students and soldiers who heard them, in contact with whose minds my own thoughts have become wider and more definite.

Not least would I thank those whose spoken and written criticisms have brought me into fuller understanding of the difficulties of thoughtful men and women of to-day. It was my original intention and promise to print the many questions sent in to me at Cambridge, with the answers given at the time. But the delay in publication, the wholly altered conditions, and the necessities of space have made it desirable to delete this part of the manuscript, and instead to endeavour to meet the substance of the more important of these criticisms in the text.

DAVID S. CAIRNS.

CONTENTS

LECTURE I

I

THE RIDDLE OF THE WORLD

THE subject on which I have been invited to address you, the problem of Christian certainty, is one of very considerable difficulty. It is a fundamental problem, and all inquiries that go to the roots of things are difficult. Moreover, the whole subject is at present in a somewhat confused and unsettled condition. One of the needs of the time is for what one may call a Critique of the Religious Reason. Much interesting material bearing upon the religious consciousness has been recently accumulated, and there are many essays and monographs about its interpretation and vindication, but there is no really great and epoch-making book upon the theme to which I can refer you as a satisfactory authority. Yet there is great need for such a book, for the

problem of certainty presses itself to-day
upon every inquiring and religious mind.
I question if there has ever been a time
when there was so great a variety of
conflicting opinions about the deepest
things as there is to-day, and many of
you, coming up to such a great intellectual centre as Cambridge University,
must have felt as if the attainment of
certainty were impossible.

In these addresses I wish to deal mainly
with the acutest form of uncertainty, with
doubt, not so much about the specific
doctrines of Christianity as about what
underlies those doctrines. All of us here,
whether we know it or not, are touched
with the faithlessness of our time, its want
of faith in the power and reality of the
Spirit. But with some this is present in
an acute and conscious form. They have
completely lost hold on the great faiths,
which they once held as dogmas, having
received them by tradition and authority.
Therefore I think that I shall best meet

the wishes of you all by beginning at the beginning, and dealing with the very bases of all religious certainty. I wish to speak to those who are out on the great waters.

But before I go further I should like to give three practical counsels to those on whom this uncertainty has laid its paralysing grasp. If you wish to have a faith that you will not need to carry, because it carries you, you must not seek certainty, you must seek truth. Having begun that inquiry, moreover, you must carry it through. Truth and certainty as to truth lie on the other side of such honest labour of the mind. I do not suppose that there is any religious teacher now living, of any intellectual range, who has not had to pass through just such a phase of uncertainty as that in which you stand at this moment. Let me read to you here the words of a great scholar of your own university which are as true to-day as when they were written.

' It is from the credulity of Christians
that the Christian faith suffers most in days
of debate, and it is well when any who
might have helpfully maintained its cause
among their neighbours, had they not been
disabled by too facile acquiescence, are im-
pelled to plunge into the deep anew. There
is not indeed, and cannot be, any security
that they shall emerge on the Christian
side. In human minds truth does not
always win a present victory even when it
is faithfully pursued. But whatever be
the present result to themselves or to
others through them, it is not possible
that they or that any should fall out of
the keeping of Him who appointed the
trial ; and to the Church any partial
loss that may arise is outweighed by the
gain from those whose faith has come
to rest on a firmer foundation. Truth
cannot be said to prevail where it is
assented to on irrelevant or insufficient
grounds, and the surest way to set free
its power is to encourage the strenuous

confronting of it with personal life and knowledge.'[1]

The second counsel is this. Be quite sure that the Christianity you feel compelled to abandon is real and essential Christianity. Nothing is more tragically evident in popular rationalistic writings of to-day than that their writers have a belated and perverted conception of the religion that they are seeking to destroy. The writers never seem to have taken the pains to find out what Christianity is. They are content with what they have been taught in their childhood, or with the representation of it given by some prominent personality or teacher. Often the reader is compelled to say, 'If that be Christianity I should agree with you. But you are fighting a shadow. You are hopelessly out of date, because you have never really seen or understood that eternal thing, the vision of which makes a man 'a Christian.' Under the limits of our

[1] Hort's *The Way, the Truth, and the Life.* (Macmillan.)

inquiry here we cannot go fully into the
question of what essential Christianity is.
I trust, however, that the outlines of that,
at least, will emerge before I have done.
I am concerned here with the two great
religious questions of our time—God and
Nature, and God and Christ.

The third counsel is one which leads at
once to the heart of our theme. It is that
we must labour to get a complete view of
the whole subject. It is, for instance, impossible to state the case for or against
Christianity until we know what religion
is, and impossible to understand what
religion is until we understand the fundamental problem of human life and destiny.

Now, to begin the real subject, let me
assume that there are those here who have
either decisively abandoned Christian faith,
or are on the eve of abandoning it. What
must be said to such men and women is,
that now they have a much greater problem
on their hands, the eternal riddle of the
world. Christianity professes to be a solu-

tion of that riddle. By abandoning it we do not therefore get rid of mystery and difficulty, but we greatly accentuate them. The riddle which had been held off and masked by Christianity stands now before us like the sphinx, ready to destroy and devour us. What is that riddle?

It is that Nature has produced a being nobler than herself. She has brought him into life, and now she seems to be incessantly seeking at once to nurture and to destroy him. What satisfactory explanation can possibly be given of a riddle like this? Let us look at the problem point by point.

First of all, I presume that no one will question that we come right out of the heart of Nature, and that at every moment we seem to be sustained by her in being. Much of the scientific labour of last century has been devoted to showing how innumerable are the bonds between the life of man and the nature world. To demonstrate this was the great work of Darwin, and his successors have applied his conceptions in every department of human life and knowledge. It is unnecessary, nowadays, to go into this in any detail, as the intimacy of the bond between Nature and man is everywhere recognised. Not only has man this nature element interwoven with his whole being, but it is also true that she is in effect a good foster-mother to us all. She is in the main still plainly beneficent to us so long as we live in conformity with her laws. We all recognise that, though they may not be the highest gifts, such natural endowments are good things to possess. And, further, every normal mind recognises the worth for life of the gifts of the nature without us, the riches of the fertile harvest field, the iron in the mine, the marble in the quarry, the half-known forces in the electron and the ether. Moreover, the appeal of Nature to our whole imaginative and spiritual side reveals a deep and vital kinship between the Nature without us and the Nature within—

we delight in her glory and wonder. Sometimes the fascination of the great mother is so intense that we can think of nothing else but the sheer magical beauty of things, the ancient woods, the sanctuaries of the mountains, 'the silence that is in the starry sky,' 'the immeasurable laughter of the sea.' We instinctively feel that the Nature that awakens this delight in us has some deep and subtle kinship with us, that we have a wonderful mother, whom we cannot choose but love.

We come out of Nature then, and draw much of our life from her still.

Yet, when all is said, in every noble human personality Nature has produced a being higher than herself.

Nature cannot think—she cannot love—she seems to have no conscience. Her mighty course is determined at all points—she is not free. By imagination and for economy of thought we personify her, but all the while the cooler reason within us knows that she is a system and not a person.

When once we have realised this we know in our souls that weak as we are in her presence she is of a lower grade than we, that we contain in us that which is of more worth than all her force and charm and terrible grandeur.

Nature is of less value than humanity, the body than the soul.

I shall return to this crucial decision later. Meantime it is enough to say that when a man comes into contact with the great ideal world he knows that he is of a higher order than the world of Nature around him.

Finally, the riddle becomes more perplexing still when we discover that the world of Nature seems to be continually seeking to overwhelm and destroy the personality which has been born from her. I have dwelt on the things in Nature which compel us to believe in her friendliness to man, but it is the sheerest sentimentality to gloss over the tremendous array of facts which may be brought forward on the other side.   This sinister side of Nature works itself out in every human tragedy. One cannot get very far on in life without being confronted by it.   Darwin has shown us how deeply inwoven in the web of life is the element of struggle and pain, that it is no accident, but essential apparently to the very constitution of Nature.   I say nothing here, however, about the tragic element in Nature.   We are concerned with it here simply in the realm of humanity. But the nature tragedy is taken up into the human life.   The first struggle for existence of primitive man was with the wild beasts, and the result was the hunting period of civilisation.   To-day one great part of the same struggle is the fight with disease, which we now know to be due for the most part to wild beasts in the organism.   Why has Nature made her children so that they prey upon one another?

The struggle for existence, moreover, is taken up into the life of nations, and results in war between nations.   Nations have come into being because they have been able to establish a covenant between the warring groups of which they were once composed. But within that covenant we have still this struggle in the form of industrial competition with all its evils. And into the whole struggling life of society the destroying powers of Nature come breaking ever and again. Messina earthquakes, *Titanic* disasters, Indian famines—these things are wrought by the Nature that seems so great and fair. She has wrought these terrible things in man in our day, and shows no repentance. She will certainly do them again. Has she not decreed love, and also—death ? Does not this tremendous discord come echoing down all time ? Are not both love and death essential to Nature as we know her ? More sinister by far is it that Nature seems to war against character as well as against happiness. If misery always produced goodness, it would be another matter. If all those struck by disease were made patient and brave thereby, it would throw light on the problem of disease of the body. But it is not true. All are not so spiritualised by suffering. Further, the nature element within us is what often makes our worst danger. The very qualities that have enabled species of animals and races of men to survive and become populous and dominant are often our worst temptations and obstacles to a higher life, when a bare existence has been won, and the new motive is to attain nobler existence. Nature seems to be our friend up to a certain point, and then to turn against us, as if she had made a nobler thing than herself, become jealous of it, and tried to arrest its further growth and destroy it.

What nobler gift of Nature is there than genius, and yet how terrible a foe of the higher life of man genius perverted can be, let history answer?

'O dumb be passion's stormy rage,
    When he who might
Have lighted up and led his age
    Falls back in night!'

Such thoughts lead us to see how dark and profound is the mystery of human life. 'All this,' says Newman, 'is a vision to dizzy and appal; and inflicts upon the mind the sense of a profound mystery which is absolutely beyond human solution.'[1] It is surely a most significant thing that the greatest poets working at white heat on the substance of human life produce not comedies but tragedies, *Prometheus*, *Œdipus*, *The Troades*, *Hamlet*, *Othello*, *Lear*, and *Faust*; that the greatest histories are those two which, penned by Thucydides and Gibbon, tell of the going down of the sun of Athens and the decline and fall of Imperial Rome; and that the greatest philosophies, whether in India, in Greece, or in Germany,[2] seek to show that the true explanation of Nature is not found in herself at all, that she, with all her glory

[1] *Apologia pro Vita Sua*, chap. v.

[2] The three great idealistic systems of history, the Indian Vedanta, Platonism, and Transcendentalism, are all at one in describing the nature world as only apparent, and in putting reality elsewhere.

and beauty and terror and pain is an apparent and a transient life, and that the true home and abiding reality of the things of beauty and love is behind and above her in the Unseen. In all this we have surely an implicit judgment of ' this present world.'

Whether the work is done by poet or sage, it is in grappling with this fundamental problem that they expend all their mightiest powers. You will never understand Christianity unless you grasp the fact that it is the greatest endeavour of all time to meet this great constant human problem, and that in abandoning it you come right up against the great darkness with which you have now to deal alone. It is vitally necessary that we should now face this vast problem that threatens all our highest existence, and all that humanity holds most dear, that we should brace all our powers and gaze steadily into the darkness.

There is a story of one of our Scottish

scholars of last generation, who had been listening to a very eloquent discourse on the life to come which dwelt in much detail of the happiness of heaven. He was asked by the preacher what he thought of it. At first he was unwilling to speak, but at last he said: 'It was very pretty, but for me one steady look into the dark is worth a hundred of your farthing candles.' The first necessity for us all is to have courage to look steadily into the dark.

'Every man has his lampful, his lampful of oil,
He may dull its glimmer by sorrow or toil;
For mine, it shall burn, with a fearless flame,
In front of the darkness that has no name.'

But courage and steadfastness, though they may lead us further, are in themselves no solution of the problem. Stoicism strengthened individuals, but it could not redeem the world. That was reserved for a religion, or rather for One Who is the centre of His religion, the greatest optimist of history Who faced the darkness, and Who none the less taught absolute faith in God and absolute love to man, and Who alone has set Hope as one of the supreme virtues between Faith and Love.

The fact may introduce us now to the thought with which we shall close this first part of our discussion, that religion historically recorded is, throughout, one sustained endeavour to grapple with this fundamental problem of the world and the soul. It must be clear to every one who thinks that the problem which I have indicated is primarily a practical problem, and only derivatively an intellectual one.

For instance, when men are plague-stricken, their first problem is how they are to get well again, and this has set them to solve the intellectual problem of disease. The latter historically grows out of the former. Now, so is it with the problem of destiny. Man's primary concern is, How am I to overcome the world ? Out of this springs the intellectual problem, ' How am I to understand the world ? '

Religion is only understood when we see it as the agelong and worldwide endeavour to grapple victoriously with the great riddle. So much, I think, has been established by the new science of Religion.

There are some indeed who demur wholly to the idea that there is any science of Religion at all. 'Do you call this thing a science,' they say, 'this immense jungle of beliefs and rituals and legends which you have accumulated, and of which every great exponent of the science has some fresh account to give?' The criticism is not without ground, and yet if one persists in the study of the science of Religion, one does find at last order coming out of chaos. One finds it possible and then necessary to classify the religions in certain ways, great constant elements appearing persistently, and, finally, a clear conviction resulting that there is one great motive running through them all. I think that we may fairly claim that on this matter there is a growing consensus among the scholars who have made the history of religion their theme. For myself I have no doubt what in essence religion is, and what is the motive that underlies the creation of all its infinitely varied forms, from ancestor worship at one end of the scale to the highest prophetic and redemptive religions at the other.

Religion is, fundamentally, on the human side, man's protest and appeal to the Supreme against the sorrows, indignities, and sins of this present world. It is the endeavour of man, through that appeal, to unite himself with the life of that unseen and ruling world, and so to win the power from it to dominate and transmute the life of time. That is to say, in essence, religion, on the human side, is simply the sustained endeavour to meet this great human problem of the destroying Nature and the struggling personality. All religions have this at their heart. They, one and all, start from an act of faith in an unseen world which is mightier than the world of sense and time, and which is either already friendly or may be made friendly to the worshippers.

Now, further, in them all you have three great constant elements.[1] There is, first of all, the conception of an unseen ruling world. No matter whether this is envisaged as spirits, or as pantheons, or as one almighty God, it is always there. It is by far the greatest and most wonderful element in Religion. Of this we shall think presently, but I content myself now with simply noting it, and pointing out that on the truth or falsity of this conception, and its character, everything else in the religion must necessarily depend.

Then, second, in every religion there is some conception of the supreme good which the worshipper seeks to derive from Heaven. The root idea here is of an

[1] See *The Rule of Faith*, p. 183, by Prof. W. P. Paterson. (Hodder and Stoughton.)

enhancement of life which is the sovereign good of man. ' Religion,' said Sabatier, ' is a prayer for life.'

> ' 'Tis life, whereof our nerves are scant,
> Oh life, not death, for which we pant ;
> More life, and fuller, that I want.'

The gods are conceived to have this in perfection, and religion aims at sharing their life with them.

And, finally, every one of the religions without exception has its own way or means of uniting the worshipper with God or the gods. Some attempt this by ritual and some by law, but it is always present. These, I repeat, are constants, and they are present in Christianity as well as in Animism. Indeed, you cannot repeat a Christian psalm or hymn without coming on one or both or all of them. We shall never, in fact, understand Christianity until we see it in the stupendous frame of world religion. I shall content myself now with simply noting these constant elements, and passing on to the next point, the universality of religion and the conclusion that follows from that universality.

The next great achievement of the science of religion is that it has demonstrated that religion is practically a universal thing. Wherever you get human nature, you may count on finding some one or other religion. Whenever you begin the study of some new race, you may be quite sure that in the history of that race you will find religion playing a great part. You cannot moreover go anywhere throughout the world to-day without finding a religion. I think that, to speak generally, that is admitted to-day by almost all competent scholars. It is quite true that you will find occasional controversy among etymologists and students of the science of Religion, as to whether this or that tribe can be said to have a religion. But these sporadic cases, which are still in dispute, are to all intent negligible in the vast human consensus. They can be easily accounted for, even if you admit that they really exist.

Further, it is no doubt true that to-day you get not only individuals but whole classes in whom the religious sense seems to have wellnigh disappeared. Take, for instance, the case of the German Social Democracy of to-day, where you have millions of men and women professing Atheism. But when you analyse the causes which have produced this state of matters, you find that the real motive of this negation is that the Social Democrat has, rightly or wrongly, become convinced that religion is bound up with the interests of the governing classes, the supporters of things as they are, and being in profound revolt against that established order of society he has for the time become utterly alienated from religion as hostile to the interests of his class. Plainly, such a state of things is due to exceptional local causes. We can easily imagine men becoming similarly alienated from art, and flung into opposition to morality because they had met only with perverted and reactionary forms of these. We must see these abnormal things in their context, and, also, in their true proportions. They are in fact almost as nothing in presence of the immense part which religion has played in human life from the very dawn of history down to the present hour. A great scholar has summed up the position by saying that ' Man is incurably religious.' Religion may die down for a time, but it always flames up again. It may become perverted and so flung into disastrous antagonism to the moral consciousness. The invariable result of that is the temporary opposition of high-minded men who repudiate all religion. But it always slowly recovers itself, and comes back again in irresistible power. It is an inveterate thing in man. ' Man is incurably religious.' The science of Religion has, I believe, established this for good and all.

But if it be so, we must make the transition from its universality to its necessity. An endowment like this cannot be accidental, it must be essential to full human nature. We must, in fact, rank it with the sense of beauty, the artistic endowment of man, out of which comes all art. We say that if a man has no sense of beauty he is abnormal. Such men and such classes of men there are, but they are by universal consent exceptions which prove the rule that art is essential to a full human life. So, too, we must rank religion in this regard with morality. There are abnormal men here also, men who have little or no sense of conscience and duty, but we are all agreed that they are abnormal, that man at his fullest and highest is an ethical being. So is it with religion. That seems to me to be substantiated at the outset by this massive consensus of the human race as to religion.

There is something very wonderful about this vast spectacle of human religion.

It is that deep and imperious instinct of the souls of men which leads them with such extraordinary persistency to affirm the existence of a world which is utterly unseen, and which yet is the real and governing world. Here we have a great venturing out of the human spirit in all ages and in all lands into a country whither the senses cannot carry it, which yet it divines to be almighty and friendly to its deepest life.

What are we to make of this venture? We may attempt to cheapen it by saying that it is pure imagination. Surely, it may be said, you are making too much of what is really a kind of poetry and folk-lore. Men and women, however, do not die for folk-lore. The extraordinary thing is not that the human mind has imagined such a world, but that it believes in it with such passion and determination, stakes its dearest upon its existence, and for its sake will give self and kindred, and even face the wreck of fatherland. There

is something more than primitive metaphysics and poetry here. There is a
passionate conviction that this world exists,
and that to find it is life, and to miss it
death. In the face of the facts of religious
history this criticism of it is mere trifling.
I say that this conviction, as it lies before
us in the marvellous story of religion, is
a wonderful spectacle. Think of the in-
timidating power of Nature—earthquake,
thunder, and tempest, and you will realise
the wonder of the undying and universal
conviction that, in spite of all appearances,
the real power lies in the Invisible, that the
Unseen is absolutely sovereign over it all. Is
this a delusion? Surely if it is a delusion
there is no instinct that we can trust.

If a persistent universal conviction like
this can be delusive, what are we to make
of moral conviction? I shall endeavour
in the next address to show that we must
hold this fundamental intuition of right
and wrong to be true. Meantime, do we not
find something in the earlier stages of life,

long before the religious instinct came into
being, which prefigures it, and leads us to see
in it the same vital impulse which is behind
the whole vast process of Evolution ?   I
shall quote here from one of your strongest
and subtlest thinkers[1]: 'And now if we
take a wider sweep and glance back at the
history of the organic world describing it,
if you will, analogically, in terms of experience rather than in the language of biology
—in which, however, such terms are more
or less covertly implied—the parable will
not be uninstructive.   We shall find that
almost every forward step in the progress
of life could be formulated as an act of
faith—an act not warranted by knowledge—on the part of the pioneer who
first made it.   There was little, for example,
in all that the wisest fish could know, to
justify the belief that there was more
scope for existence on the earth than in
the water, or to show that persistent
endeavours to live on land would issue

[1] J. Ward, *Realm of Ends*, pp. 415-416, ed. 1911.

in the transformation of his swim-bladder into lungs. And before a bird had cleaved the air there was, surely, little in all that the most daring saurian speculators could see or surmise concerning that untrodden element, to warrant him in risking his neck in order to satisfy his longing to soar ; although, when he did try, his forelimbs were transformed to wings at length, and his dim prevision of a bird became incarnate in himself. So put, these instances will seem largely fanciful, I am well aware, too Lamarckian even for Lamarck. Still they serve to bring out the one fact, viz. that when we regard the development of living forms as a continuous whole, we are forced to recognise as immanent and operative throughout it, a sort of unscientific trustfulness that seems to have been engrained in all living things.' Dr. Ward adds the application, which I doubt not has already suggested itself to you. 'This trustfulness, might I say, is comparable to the faith of Abraham who,

when he was called to go out to a place
which he should after receive for an inheritance, obeyed and went out, not knowing whither he went.' I would extend
that application still further, and say
that it is comparable to that profoundly
impressive trustfulness in the Unseen,
which lies behind the entire history of
human religion.

Just as plant and beast and bird have
progressed by venturing forth into a
new environment, so man has taken the
still more daring step of launching himself
out into a new world. The vital intuition
which has led him to this seems to me
quite the most wonderful thing in human
nature, the thing for which all the lower
stages of life exist, the culmination of
Evolution. It must be toward this that
life all the way up has been struggling.
For this the strata have been piled, for
this the civilisations have been reared and
sunk again, for this the generations lavished
on land and sea. And to-day its purifica-

tion and development in the human race is the central interest in history. I believe that all the material and secular elements in human life are but scaffolding for the house of Faith.

I do not doubt myself that this wonderful power of the soul is as yet but in its infancy, and that when it is full grown the world of which it gives us glimpses will be more real to us than the earth dream in which we live. If this surmise be true, it follows that you and I are already living in the eternal world, that all around us there is an ocean of beauty and life and love in God ; that we are as much in eternity to-night as we ever shall be, though one day we shall know it better. It means that in that infinite world there are for us all hidden springs of joy and power, to partake of which will give us strength to solve the great riddle of the world, and so to overcome that world that, in the light of that victory, shared at last by all mankind, we shall see that all the long battle and anguish and toil were worth while, inasmuch as they drove man to make the great discovery of God and of the life everlasting. All that is involved in this conception of Faith.

But you may say, ' What is this Faith ? ' I can make nothing of it if it is not a power of immediate consciousness of the eternal world.

It may be said, ' That is impossible. What you have already admitted about the history of religion contradicts it. If men are endowed with such a power, why are their reports of the unseen world in such glaring disagreement? The whole story of religious conceptions, with their dissolving pantheons, is much liker a nightmare than a real and solid world.'

In answer I would say, first of all, that I do not look upon faith as resembling a mathematical intuition, something which you discern as you do an axiom. It is rather like a gradually developing consciousness comparable to a man's growing sense of beauty or of honour. The objection taken alone might in fact be urged with equal force against any idealistic view of art or of ethics.

Two or three years ago I spent a morning in the great gallery of sculpture in Athens. The creations of Greek genius are there arranged in historical series. They begin with the grotesque grinning faces and rigid forms of the primitive period, which remind one of the wooden dolls of one's childhood. It is profoundly interesting to watch there the gradual awakening of the sense of beauty in the Greek mind, to see those grinning masks gradually becoming instinct with expression, and those rigid forms full of life and grace. At last comes the great hour when like a flash the heavenly beauty is born— creative genius flames into splendour and burns, and shines. But the divine inspiration fades gradually away, and you see the faces becoming inexpressive and the forms conventional again, though not on the first low plane.

Now, does the fact that the Greek sense of beauty fluctuated imply that beauty is a purely subjective thing—that there is nothing in the world without corresponding to the artistic vision? I should say rather that you cannot understand the supreme works of the Greek masters (or any of the great masters of beauty) unless you recognise that there is an objective standard of beauty which does not change, and which is embodied in the works of the great Athenian prime more perfectly than in the primitive and later conventional sculpture. We have a colloquial expression which brings this out. We look at certain second-rate pictures, and then come on something by a greater hand. We say: 'Ah, that is the real thing!' Something eternal in us recognises the eternal in the world without. So we speak of genius as creative. Something of reality is brought out of the unseen and embodied here. So in that gallery one seems to see the Hellenic mind struggling as it were with a dream, and then for one brief and glorious hour coming broad awake to the perfect beauty, and then slowly falling into the duller dream of it again; haunted this time by memories of the fairer world to which for a little it had awakened. Do we not get the same kind of thing in the moral sphere? As we study the fluctuating moral conceptions of mankind, do we not get precisely the same dizzying sense of phantasmagoria as the pantheons give us in Comparative Religion. Yet we, surely, cannot doubt that Duty, Honour, Love and Truth have in them the unchanging substance of eternity. Here, too, our sense of these realities may fluctuate, but they themselves do not change.

The earth dream may prevail for ages, but now and again men and nations become broad awake and discern with piercing clearness the things 'that cannot be bought with

a price, and that do not die with death.'
So is it, I repeat, with the religious sense,
the conviction of the reality and the power
of the Unseen World. That perception
may change, it may come and go, but in
its essence while it survives it is waking
vision, it is the immediate consciousness
of the Living God.

LECTURE II

II

FAITH

In the last address we saw that if we abandon Christianity because we find its problems insoluble, we have at once a far vaster problem on our hands, the riddle of the world. We saw that the science of Religion had made it clear that religion, universally regarded, was on its human side an attempt to solve that riddle by enabling men to transcend and so to overcome the world. We saw that the point from which all religions started was the conviction that above and behind the present world there was another and a mightier universe, a spiritual and unseen world, by union with which men could attain the life and freedom which in their fulness were denied them here.

41

At heart all religions have this common motive, Christianity among the rest. What the relation of Christianity is to these other religions is a question which we shall reserve till the last address. Meantime we are concerned with the basal question of how far religion really faces and solves the great riddle. Clearly, the vital point here is as to whether the greater spiritual order which it professes to reveal really exists, and whether we can know its character. All religion makes this great hypothesis. Is it only a hypothesis? Is it valid? These questions raise the whole problem of religious knowledge, and of its origin, Faith. We have already seen that the universality and the inveteracy of religion make it almost incredible that the whole is an illusion, that there is no real substance in it. To adventure on an enterprise like that is to commonsense as desperate as to deny that there is any enduring substance in art or in morality. If religion is purely subjective illusion, so may they be. I admit that we have only made a beginning when we have said this, but it is a substantial beginning, which determines our whole later course of thought. For if religion be more than a subjective illusion, if there really be such a vast and omnipotent spiritual world transcending and yet interpenetrating our life of sense and time, then the power in us of discerning that world, whether we call it instinct, sense, consciousness or intuition, is a very wonderful thing. It must, indeed, be the greatest endowment of human nature. It is with a very deep sense, therefore, of the moment of our theme that I approach the subject of Faith. In my belief, there is involved in it the whole question of whether there is a Living God, and whether we can come into present relations with Him.

It may be said, ' Do you really stake that supreme interest on Faith ? ' Why do you not rather go into the metaphysical arguments for His Being, the Theistic

proofs of the text-books, and the external
evidences of Christianity? I take this
view, first of all, for the reason that those
proofs are, one and all, after-thoughts.
They were wrought out for the purpose of
demonstrating to the speculative reason
a conviction which came into the world by
a different road. It was not in this way
that belief in the Living God came to men
at all. There is no doubt whatever as to
this. It is perfectly certain that the great
main stream of faith in the Living God
which flows through human life to-day
came through the Hebrew people. Its
fountain was in the history of Israel, in
what is known as the Old Testament revelation. This is, of course, true of Christen-
dom, and it is practically certain also
that the stern monotheism of Islam came
out of Judaism, and therefore had the
same source as the monotheism of Christianity.

Now, we have the processes of the
Hebrew mind laid open to us in the

Old Testament writings, and, as every careful student of these writings knows, there is in them hardly the slightest trace of any dialectical reasoning as to the being of God. The Old Testament writers, historians, psalmists, and prophets came to be very sure of God by quite different ways from the laborious processes of the older apologetic text-books. Faith came to them along another channel. It is my belief that that channel is open now, and may become more open still. In what follows I shall try to indicate that course, in order that having discovered it we may clear it where it is choked, and let the living waters flow. Be it noted, however, in passing, that I am not here disparaging or even criticising the Theistic proofs. If a man can strengthen his belief in God by them, as I believe he can, that is all to the good. I only wish to make it quite clear that those conclusions which he seeks to verify by them were, to begin with, reached by humanity along the tracks I am seeking to open up with you now, by Faith and by Revelation.

I have already referred to the criticism that there cannot be in us a valid faculty of Faith, because the things which it discloses to us about God are so contradictory. How can there be true vision of God, inhering in the soul of man when the history of religion shows us such contradictions? Sometimes the unseen world is viewed as populated by a host of spirits, sometimes it is envisaged as a Valhalla, and again as an Olympus. And even within the history of the same religion the pantheons change as in a kaleidoscope. We see the gods of the Vedas, for instance, change into the pantheon of Hinduism. That is perfectly true, but there is something constant amid all the flux, as I have endeavoured to show, and that constant is the supremely significant thing.

Always there is the idea of the ruling spiritual world. But there is something

more to be said. What that is I think I
can best bring out by an illustration.
When you are writing a poem, let us say,
you come ever and again to the point
where you feel that you have not got the
right word. (I have had that experience
frequently in delivering these lectures!)
Note what goes on in your mind as you
search for the missing word. Word after
word comes up, and you try each as it
comes, rejecting them one by one until the
right one appears, and in a flash is recognised and chosen. There is something in
your mind obviously which is seeking for
its right expression, and which has what
Lotze calls a ' protective ' power which
makes it refuse what does not belong to
it, and then to claim its own.

Something like that I believe is true of
the great common mind of humanity.
In the history of religion we see it as it
were concentrated on this supreme interest,
the existence and character of this ruling
spiritual world, and trying to envisage it

in god after god, and pantheon after pantheon, creating and dissolving them, but always recurring anew to the task. Sometimes there is a twilight of all the gods, or even, as in Buddhism, a complete eclipse, or a Ragnarök or *Götterdämmerung*. But that does not last, the remorseless something behind them all in the mind that has refused them all is not content with vacuity and negation, but persists, and so the task is taken up again and again, the endless task of seeking after God. 'O God,' said Augustine, ' Thou hast made us for Thyself, and our heart is restless until it find rest in Thee.'

It may be said that, after all, this does not take us very far. After all, you have only got this eternal unseen almighty world which either is, or may be made, friendly to the worshipper. But you really have more. You have the invariable human sense of kinship with that world witnessed by the desire to share its life. Further, you have that world invariably conceived of as fundamentally personal. That is really involved in the sense of kinship. Philosophy finds endless difficulty here, and often tries to sublimate this conviction away, but so far as religion is concerned, the effort always fails. The religious mind cannot exist if you destroy this sense of kinship somehow existing with the Unseen. But within those limits there are wide differences, from the swarm of spirits and the remoter hierarchy of higher gods of the Animist up to the vividly imagined polytheism of East and West.

The next step taken by the expanding religious consciousness of mankind was to unify the pantheon. The remorseless thing in the soul of man that was seeking expression knew that these pantheons did not express the deepest in it. The poets might give the consecration of their genius to the legends of the gods, the priests might rivet the dominion of the past by every device of craft, and by appealing to every passion of lust or avarice or fear, but they could not satisfy or silence that deep vital passion

for truth about the eternal. The noblest
men felt that a strong and worthy moral
life could not be won in servitude to
many gods. You might conciliate one,
but who could be safe from the jealousy
and anger of the rest? What unity and
strength of life could be won with such
an account of the ultimate things? But
the battle for unity was long and hard, and
the advance to Monotheism was one of
the greatest of all victories of the higher
life of mankind.

Historically it came through one little
people inhabiting a mountain land in the
Eastern Mediterranean. We cannot go
here into the great story of how the God
of the tribe became for the Hebrew the
One God who created the heavens and the
earth. That is one of the most wonderful
histories in all the world, that story of the
leaping forward of the awakening soul
of man to the great truth of the unity of
God. The whole future of humanity lay in
that discovery. It was accompanied and

followed by another which was equally vital, the conviction that this one Almighty God was absolutely righteous. The two victories were really one and the same.

Hitherto men had thought of the gods very much as magnified men like themselves, who might be persuaded or bribed by offerings and service to forward their cause. On the whole they were regarded as the guardians of the existing moralities which were part of the contract between the nations and their divinities. But to identify God with goodness was an epoch-making advance. This, as I have said, was in its completeness the achievement of Hebrew prophecy. Cornill has called Amos 'the most wonderful phenomenon in the history of the human spirit.' Whether that be true or not of Amos it is true of Hebrew prophecy. Outside of the Christian revelation there is nothing to compare with it in the story of the soul of man.

'All that you can conceive of impartial

righteousness, and of forgiving love, that,'
said the prophets, 'is true of the one
Almighty God.' There is a life-or-death
leap of the soul of man out into that great
unknown ruling world, an intuition that
fills one with wonder at its boldness. To
unite religion with morality is to begin a
new world.

Now, was that moralising of religion a
sound and reasonable step to take?

When we ask that question we leave
history, and, face to face with the riddle of
the world, we ask for ourselves if this is a
real solution—valid for us to-day. Was this
bold new venture of the human spirit out
into the vast dim unseen world a disastrous error, or a profound intuition of
reality? You will never face a greater
question than this, though you live to all
eternity. It is really the question as to
whether Force or Right is the ultimate
thing in the universe, and that in the end
of the day is the question as to whether
in the end humanity will exterminate

itself, or climb to undreamed-of heights
of nobility and joy.

Let us face the issues. There is not one
human being here who does not find in
himself two worlds of motive. There is
the world that we have taken over from
the nature process, the survival in us of the
ape and tiger, and, as Bishop Creighton
said, of the primeval donkey, too! Then
intertwined with that, but stretching beyond it, there is the world which conscience
reveals, the ideal world. It is part of our
complete humanity that we have to live
in both worlds. We need the lower as well
as the higher so long as we live in sense
and time. Some of this nature life within
us is better worth keeping than the rest,
and so we appraise it according to certain
relative standards of less and greater
value. But it is quite otherwise with
the other world. Its standards are absolute. We have no right to sell justice or
truth for anything in the lower realm.
We know that righteousness and goodness

are of intrinsic and absolute value, and that their pursuit is imperative on all spirits of men.

These convictions are elemental and ultimate. I cannot prove them to you if you do not believe them. I can only express my conviction that my personality would go to pieces if I did not hold to them, and that it would be a good thing if it did. It would not be worth keeping.

Let me quote here a passage from an early volume on Theism by an old teacher of my own, whose words carry weight wherever philosophy is studied: 'The divine must be held to be the most fully and adequately revealed in the highest aspects of our experience. If again, we are asked how we distinguish between what is higher and lower, it is clear that no formal or merely intellectual test such as "growing complexity of detail harmonised within a single whole" will suffice. This may be a characteristic of the higher stages, but, clearly, the realisation of an

abstract formula like this possesses in itself no interest or value. It is the extent
of any experience which makes it higher
in any vital sense, and makes it of decisive
importance as throwing light on the meaning of experience as a whole. And in any
such estimate we must ultimately rest
our whole case on an absolute judgment
of value. Man, says Kant, is in his
typically rational activities, an end in
himself. The life, that is to say, which
is guided by the ideals of truth, beauty,
and goodness, and which partially realises
these, possesses an absolute and indefeas-
ible worth. Such a judgment represents a
conviction so deep that we are prepared to
stake everything upon it. Strictly speaking, such a conviction is not the result of
argument, or a deduction from any philo-
sophic system. It might rather be spoken
of as an assumption, the fundamental
assumption upon which all subsequent
philosophising must depend. Without
this assumption of the infinite value and

significance of human life, argument about God is simply waste of time. The man who does not start from this assumption —the man who can embrace the opposite alternative—is not accessible to any argument. . . . He has denied his calling, or as Fichte puts it, he has elected to be a thing and not a person. Of such an one it can only be said, He is joined to his idols : let him alone. Faith in God can only rest securely on the basal certainty of duty, and the view of human destiny and the universal purpose that spring therefrom.' [1]

I entirely agree with this view. When it comes to be a question of comparing personality and nature, of what is right with what is expedient, logical argument is of little use if we do not directly feel and see the sheer distinction between intrinsic and relative worth. ' We rest the whole case on a simple judgment of value.' We can never get that which is

---

[1] *Two Lectures on Theism*, by Prof. A. Pringle Pattison, pp. 62-64. (Blackwood.)

higher out of any combination of what is
lower. It is here that we break out of
the subjective and relative into what is
objective and absolute. Duty is the
rock in the maelstrom where we can take
our stand. Many a man, who in these
bewildering and testing days has given up
every form of faith, stands fast in this
recognition of the immutable difference
between right and wrong. The great
house of Faith in which his fathers wor-
shipped may be down, the wild elemental
forces of storm and earthquake may
have shattered it, the winds may be sweep-
ing through the ruins, the wild grass
growing where the altar stood. But if
that one shrine stands, and if he can keep
the light burning there, then I believe
that either in this life or in some life
which is to come, the whole of that ancient
world of faith will come back again in
nobler form than before. If you will
persist in staking your life on that conviction, the logic of the years will over-

bear the logic of the hours, and bring you
back at last to faith in God, and, I believe,
to faith in God in Christ.

It is here that, for my part, I get out
of this haunting difficulty about subjec-
tivity, for I know when I am face to face
with the moral imperative that I am
dealing with a world which is not relative
but absolute, that does not depend on
me and human beings like me for its
existence, but that is in truth a world on
which I and all men depend. But you
cannot possibly get this judgment of
intrinsic worth, and this moral imperative which is involved in it, out of the
cosmic process. Huxley in his Romanes
Lecture has put in its classical form that
insoluble problem of all Naturalism, that
problem which we have seen to lie behind
all religion, that Nature has produced a
being higher than herself, and that, now
she has produced him, she is seeking constantly to destroy him. What you find
in that famous lecture, which has been

called the swan song of Naturalism, is the
profoundly impressive statement of the
conviction that it is utterly impossible to
derive human morality from the cosmic
process, inasmuch as that process is obviously flagrantly unmoral. I refer to
Huxley's view, not because it is complete,
but because it emphasises, no doubt in an
extreme way, those elements in Nature
which all admit to be present in her,
elements which compel the belief that she
is not co-extensive with the whole of
things. Man, says Huxley, has to build up
within that vast process his little human
world of duty and kindness and commonsense, as a man reclaims a garden from
the wild moor, or builds a hothouse for
his exotics in a northern clime. But let
him not think that he is building according to Nature, for in truth he is building
out of his own soul. So Huxley endeavours
to maintain the moral values in an unmoral
cosmos. It is no doubt true that Huxley,
like Darwin, has over-emphasised the dark

side of Nature. This has in particular been shown in a number of books and articles, by Geddes and Thomson in their volume on the *Evolution of Sex*, by Kropotkin in his volume on *Mutual Aid*, by Henry Drummond in *The Ascent of Man*, and by Professor J. Arthur Thomson most recently in his striking pamphlet on *Biology and War*,[1] where a list of the recent literature is given.

If a layman in science may venture an opinion, the case has clearly been made out for a larger and more generous interpretation of the ways of Nature than the darker early view. It would almost seem as if Nature became liker a moral order as she drew near her crowning work. I do not know that we can go further than that, nor do I think that these distinguished writers claim more. Taking the Nature system, as a whole, it seems to include both the self-regarding struggle and the struggle for the life of others, both egoism and altruism.

[1] Published by Humphrey Milford. Oxford University Press.

But I believe we need much more than this if we are really to maintain the existence of intrinsic moral values. We need a spiritual world which underlies Nature, and for whose manifestation in time Nature is a preparation. But in truth the effort is a hopeless one on the terms which he lays down. For when all is said, the fundamental thing is the cosmic process and the 'Veiled Power' behind it.[1] It is the thing out of which man and his world came, and by which they will be swallowed up at last. All human dreams of duty and of love and of beauty are like rainbows on the cataract—'unceasing thunder and eternal foam.' The judgments of intrinsic worth, the sense of an eternal law of duty are illusions. They are concomitants of physical processes, 'epiphenomena' of sense experiences.

The fundamental reality is 'unmoral.' There was thus a beginning to the moral imperative and there will be an end. The

[1] See Epilogue to this Volume.

reality and the power lie elsewhere. Now I maintain that if you strike these away from the moral imperative, you cannot permanently sustain it. It is no answer to this to point out that there are individuals who hold this dark and sad cosmology, and who maintain a noble morality none the less. The whole story of the religions of the world demonstrates that individuals are often nobler than their creed, just as they are often worse. The individual man is a strange blend of that which is transmitted through the environment, and inherited from an ancestry of faith or unfaith, and the personal thoughts which he has wrought out for himself, or is in process of working out. It is a commonplace of religious biography that no man is wholly consistent or logical in such matters, that a John Newton, for instance, may be a slave trader after he has become a convert of that evangelical revival which gave slavery in our land its death-blow. But there is for all that a

vital connection between the philosophy a
man holds and his practice, a connection
which manifests itself in the course of
the years. Generations are more logical
than individuals, and history demonstrates
the remorseless way in which through the
centuries right and wrong beliefs work
themselves out in conduct. I surely do
not need to spend time in showing from
history that men tend to become like the
God whom they believe to be at the heart
of things, whether they call Him Force
or Love. So the materialism of the middle
of last century which combined a high
morality with a naturalistic basis runs
out in a few decades to Nietzsche, with
his admiration for 'the blonde beast' who
is 'avidly rampant for spoil and victory.'
If, then, on the other hand, you hold fast
with your soul to the intrinsic moral
values, to the absolute moral imperative,
you will be led inevitably, sooner or later, to
the conviction that the universe is fundamentally moral, that it exists for moral

and spiritual ends, and you will be within
sight of the final goal of the whole process
of reasoning, that the universe has its source
and ground in ' One whom we describe
least imperfectly when we call Him Personal.' For how can we predicate intelligence and purpose and love and truth of
any impersonal being. Is not the denial
of personality here merely verbal. The
thing that the doubter thought that he
had eliminated in principle comes back
in substance in the fundamental conviction that intrinsic moral values can only
be sustained in a moral universe. A moral
universe implies a Living God.

Have we gone too fast ? If so, let us
return to the crucial point. It may be
said by some one, ' The step you take
from this inner world of the soul to the
fundamental character of this stupendous
world of nature is beyond me. It is a
leap into the unknown which I cannot
take. True knowledge comes by slower
and surer methods, by patient inductions

and demonstrations. There is something unreasonable in a sudden flight of this kind, from what goes on in the soul of a man to the essential nature of the vast universe. You have called your argument 'The Reasonableness of the Christian Faith,' but at the heart of it you are exalting what cannot be called reasonable, what in fact is a flight of imagination, rather than the demonstration which the standards of modern knowledge demand.'

What are we to say in reply to a challenge like this ? First let us sum up our conclusions so far. These are, that there is an absolute moral imperative, and that moral values are intrinsic, *i.e.* that justice and love and truth are ends in themselves and not mere utilities and expediencies. Second, that the world is a unity. Thirdly, that for the urgent·practical necessities of conduct we have to try to reach some solution of the riddle of the world, inasmuch as the sphinx will devour us if we cannot solve her problem.

E

Now, let us take an illustration.

Some years ago we had in the college in which I teach a young student of theology, a quiet, unassuming, kindly man. On the eve of our winter term I had a letter from him, telling me that he was busy preparing for it, and asking for advice as to his work. Before I could answer it, I read in the newspapers the story of his death. He had gone out one morning from his home in a little fisher town on the Moray Firth to do a forenoon's reading in a quiet spot on the links by the sea, when he saw a boy, a stranger to the place, going out into waters that he knew to be dangerous. He cried out to him to warn him, but the boy took no heed. After a while Maclean heard a cry out at sea, and looking up from his books he saw that the boy was struggling with the current. He laid his books down, made straight for the water and swam out to him, with a plank he had somehow got hold of on his way. He got up to the lad in time, and as the

current swept them both outward, tried
in vain to get him on the plank. But the
lad was exhausted, and again and again
slipped off. Then he felt his strength
giving out, but up to the very end per-
sisted, and at last succeeded, and saved
his man. But his own powers were exhausted, and he sank and was drowned.
That was a case of as deliberate self-
sacrifice as ever I have known.

I want you to realise that scene. You
have the whole nature cosmos around you
there in symbol, sky and sea and hill
and shore, and in the middle of it you
have got this deliberate laying of life
down. As you look at it you see that
this is no unconnected picture. Somehow, it is all one whole. The man could
not have given his life if it had not been
for the nature cosmos. It was the arena.
It furnished the conditions of the moral
action. Now, you have got to do one of
two things. Since it is one whole, you
have either got to interpret that act of

self-sacrifice in terms of sky and sea and
land, of Nature in short ; or else you have
got to turn the whole thing about, and
interpret sky and sea and land in relation
to this act of heroism. You have got to
make your choice, and your choice will
depend entirely on your estimate of moral
values. If you feel that you stand here
in presence of something of absolute worth,
then the only possible conclusion must be,
I believe, that somehow Nature was there
in order that the man might do this thing ;
that in actions of this kind, and the personalities that lie behind them, lies the
clue to the riddle of the world, and the
manifestation at once of the source from
which that world came, and the end
towards which it is working. If you hold
to the absolute nature of the good, then,
if you are to be reasonable, you must
sooner or later come to this conclusion.
If you take the other course, if you interpret the action and the life which expressed itself in that action, simply in

terms of Nature, then you must say that it was all a matter of instinct, part of the Nature mechanism, and only of relative value as a part of that machinery, like any other part, like the cry of the sea gulls overhead, or the murderous current that swept the man to his doom. You have got, I repeat, to make your choice between these two exclusive views. If you choose the former and carry it clear through, all the nature cosmos becomes transformed, and you will see that it is all 'co-operant to an end,' the end of producing personalities and training them in justice, love, honour and 'the things which cannot be bought with a price, and that do not die with death.'

But if you have come so far with me, I believe you must come further. In the opening lecture and the earlier part of this, we were thinking of that primitive religious intuition of the existence of an unseen ruling world which in the end of the day controlled this sense world of

Nature, an unseen world of reality and power, to which the total religious consciousness of mankind bore its immense and convincing witness. If we are to go on thinking things into a unity, there must come a moment when there comes a complete fusion of the religious and the moral consciousness, when we identify the all-powerful Being to whom the religious consciousness bears witness, with the all-good Being revealed in conscience. That is the great fundamental act of Faith in God. It is a simple immediate intuition of the presence and the nature of that Being Who created and Who sustains and governs the world. I cannot explain it in any other way than that it is a direct immediate consciousness of the presence of the Living God, into which we pass as it were by a kind of awakening from the mere life of Nature, the great sense dream of things in which we are involved by our human constitution and inheritance. If we are to understand what in

its essence faith is, we have to go to the
noblest examples of it, the utterances of
it which all men recognise as classical.
When we want to know what music is
we do not go to music-hall melodies or
gramophones, we go to Beethoven or
Bach or Wagner. Even so, when we are
inquiring as to what faith is, we must
give some account of it which will explain
so glorious an utterance of it, as, for instance, the one hundred and thirty-ninth
psalm :—

'O Lord, thou hast searched me, and known me.
 Thou knowest my downsitting and mine uprising,
 Thou understandest my thought afar off.
 Thou searchest out my path and my lying down,
 And art acquainted with all my ways.
 For there is not a word in my tongue,
 But, lo, O Lord, thou knowest it altogether.
 Thou hast beset me behind and before,
 And laid thine hand upon me.
 Such knowledge is too wonderful for me ;
 It is high, I cannot attain unto it.
 Whither shall I go from thy spirit ?
 Or whither shall I flee from thy presence ?
 If I ascend up into heaven, thou art there :
 If I make my bed in Sheol, behold, thou art there.

If I take the wings of the morning,
And dwell in the uttermost parts of the sea ;
Even there shall thy hand lead me,
And thy right hand shall hold me.
If I say, Surely the darkness shall overwhelm me,
And the light about me shall be night ;
Even the darkness hideth not from thee,
But the night shineth as the day :
The darkness and the light are both alike to thee.
For thou hast possessed my reins :
Thou hast covered me in my mother's womb.
I will give thanks unto thee ; for I am fearfully and
      wonderfully made :
Wonderful are thy works ;
And that my soul knoweth right well.
My frame was not hidden from thee,
When I was made in secret,
And curiously wrought in the lowest parts of the earth.
Thine eyes did see mine unperfect substance,
And in thy book were all my members written,
Which day by day were fashioned,
When as yet there were none of them.
How precious also are thy thoughts unto me, O God !
How great is the sum of them !
If I should count them, they are more in number
      than the sand :
When I awake, I am still with thee.
Surely thou wilt slay the wicked, O God :
Depart from me therefore, ye bloodthirsty men.
For they speak against thee wickedly,
And thine enemies take thy name in vain.

Do not I hate them, O Lord, that hate thee ?
And am not I grieved with those that rise up against
    thee ?
I hate them with perfect hatred :
I count them mine enemies.
Search me, O God, and know my heart :
Try me, and know my thoughts :
And see if there be any way of wickedness in me,
And lead me in the way everlasting.'

When you take an utterance like this, and read it with any real understanding, you cannot but feel that the unknown writer is speaking out of an overwhelming and yet liberating sense (there is no other word for it), the sense of the presence of God. No doubt there is a long history behind it, no doubt many influences have gone to the making of it, but now that it is there, it is immediate. The man has become awake to what was always there.

> ' And without a screen
> At last is seen
> The Presence in which I have always been.'

The history and the development of that sense is the history of an awakening of man.

Not all humanity awakened simultaneously. It is the supreme distinction of the Hebrew race that it awoke first to 'the Presence in which it had always been.' That is what gives the Bible its supreme place in religion. Israel awoke while Assyria and Babylon and Tyre and Sidon slumbered and clung to their dreams. Israel was the child that awoke first, and wandered out of the house into the wonderful dew-pearled dawn, and saw the mountains and the valleys shining with a strange new radiance, and felt neither lonely nor afraid because of the new Presence. But the dreamers within doors slumbered on through their drunken dreams of barbarous pantheons, Nergal and Thoth and Baal and Astarte, and thought Israel mad with its morning song of the One and Only God.

'To the other nations,' says Lotze, 'Israel seemed mad. To us to-day the Hebrews seem to have been the one sober people in a world of drunkards.' Still to-day we have the same inward evidence.

We who believe in Him know that there is a Living God. If you ask how we know, we say, ' Because He haunts us, because we cannot get away from Him ; because we would not if we could : because we feel Him, know Him, see Him.' It is an immediate consciousness, which may fluctuate and waver in a man because of his own want of prayer and obedience, but if he follow his highest and fights the world instead of yielding to it, more and more God possesses him, and he becomes broader and broader awake as the years go on.

It will be said to me perhaps, ' This is too shot through with emotion for me : it is too imaginative. I should like to believe it, but I want proof, and scientific proof.' ' To yield to emotion in the search for truth,' said Huxley once, ' is immoral.'

I would reply to that, first of all, that in stating the problem as to the actual facts on which the intuition proceeds, I have here stated realities. The riddle of

the world is a simple description of Nature
and of Personality as they are. The moral
imperative is a thing as solid, to say the
least, as sun and moon and star. I wish
now to say, further, plainly that this distinction between passionless science and
emotional and imaginative faith has been
grossly overdone. How have the great
scientific discoveries actually been made?
'Oh,' says one, 'they are made by obser-
vation, and by the strict application of
the inductive methods. The whole process is passionless and rational. The discoverer has to keep his feelings and imagination under the strictest control.' If that
were all, nothing would ever be found out.
The investigator would be smothered in
the endless multitude of facts. In truth,
to state the matter in this way is to omit
the most vital and interesting thing in
scientific method,—the birth of hypothesis. How does a man come to observe
the right things, to see the relevant fact,
to make the true hypothesis? How does

he come to choose the few, and then the one, out of the many? We may roughly define the peculiar quality that distinguishes the real discoverer from the hack and pedant as imagination. Further, to say that scientific discovery has not a profoundly emotional element in the heart of it, is utterly belied by scientific biography. If there is one thing that strikes me more than another in the story of science, it is that to be a great scientific discoverer a man needs courage. They have all been brave mariners, the men who have broken the restraining barriers and sailed out into the unknown.

> ' We were the first that ever burst
> Into that silent sea.'

If you wish to see how a great imaginative artist in marble has depicted the spirit of scientific discovery, go and look at the face of that noble statue of Newton in the antechapel at Trinity. It might be the face of some great captain at the

climax of some earth-shaking battle on
which the fortunes of centuries depend.
As he stands there looking into the unknown, he is the very picture of daring.
But where there is courage there must be
danger, and where there is danger there
must be emotion.

Further, there never yet was a discovery
made save under the sense of need of some
kind or other. Mach, a famous man of
science of our day, tells us of Mayer the
joint discoverer with Joule of the principle of the conservation of energy, that
he said, he made the discovery because
he felt the need of it.[1]

Yet again scientific biography shows
both directly and indirectly how deeply

[1] 'If, finally, you ask me how I became involved in
the whole affair, my answer is simply this : Engaged
during a sea voyage almost exclusively with the study
of physiology I discovered the new theory, for the
sufficient reason that I felt the need of it.' ' Quoted
by Mach in his *Popular Science Lectures*, p. 184, 3rd
edition (American).

See in particular Poincaré's volume on *Science and
Method*, pp. 46-63.

the feeling and the imagination are stirred by any great discovery. The evidence is sometimes indirect. It is a well-known psychological fact that in moments of high emotional tension the impressions made on the sense by outside objects are often extraordinarily deep. I can never forget, for instance, the strange livid aspect of the under side of the leaves of a laurel-bush outside the window of a room into which I had been hastily summoned to the deathbed of an acquaintance many years ago. Doubtless many of you have similar associations with scents and sounds. Some of these may be congenital and some acquired.

Sometimes the evidence is direct. Hear Darwin as he tells us of one of the discoveries which followed in the wake of the master discovery of natural selection. 'I remember the very day and spot when it came to me, in a country road near Down.'

Listen again to Alfred Russell Wallace,

his co-discoverer of the law of natural selection in the far-off East Indian Archipelago. He tells us how, during an attack of intermittent fever as he lay thinking over the problem of the origin of species, his thoughts turned to Malthus's well-known essay on Population, which he had read twelve years before. Step by step his mind moved on to the conclusion that the principles of this essay applied to all living things. ' Then it suddenly flashed upon me that this self-acting process would necessarily improve the race . . . that is, the fittest would survive. Then at once I seemed to see the whole effect of this. . . . The more I thought over it, the more I became convinced that I had at length found the long-sought-for law of nature that solved the problem of the origin of species.' [1]

Now to come closer, and to analyse the actual psychology of discovery, let me tell you an unpublished story which was told

[1] *Autobiography*, pp. 190-191. Edition 1908.

me by my friend and colleague, the late
Principal Lindsay. He said that Lord
Kelvin once told him that he had never
reasoned his way quite up to any one of
his great discoveries. He brooded over all
the facts which seemed to him relevant to
his problem, until there came a moment
when his mind took a life-or-death leap
away out into the unknown. He felt in
the very marrow of his being the conviction that the solution lay just *there*.

That this is the usual way in which
the discovering mind works in science is,
I think, pretty generally admitted to-day.
Some time ago I told this incident to
two very distinguished men of science,
both of whom I may say in passing have
been Gifford lecturers and are experts in
Biology. Both of them at once agreed in
the view that that is how discoveries
in science are always made. 'The end,'
they said, 'is seen before the means.'

But there were two further points in the
story. The first was that he was never able

F

to put in the intervening stepping-stones
of demonstration between his old position
and the new to which his life and death
spring had brought him. The other was
that he was not content to leave it there,
but before he published his discoveries
got his two friends, Tait and Clerk Maxwell,
to work out the missing deductions, to lay
down the missing stones in the stream.
There is a world of significance here for
the theory of discovery. He had leaped
beyond his powers of demonstration by
virtue of just that incalculable something
which made him first-rate, that thing which
we call genius.[1] When I heard that story
the thought came to me, How wonderfully
like this is to Faith, the spirit in man that
'goeth out not knowing whither it goeth,
because it desireth a better country, even
an heavenly,' the desire to grasp the key

[1] No comparison is, of course, suggested here between
these great men of Science. Lord Kelvin's friends had
not been pre-occupied, as he had been, with the
particular problems in question.

of the great riddle of the world, and find its way through it to God.

Faith is Intuition. Why not give it its right name ? Faith is Genius. It is genius at work on a vaster problem than any problem of science, the riddle of the world. But it is genius, mark you, that proceeds first by getting its moral values right. Until a man recognises the nature and authority of the moral imperative he has simply not got the actual facts of his world problem before him. Only the pure in heart, or those who truly desire to be pure in heart, can ever see God.

Science, moreover, is primarily concerned with fragments of the mighty whole of things, but Faith is always concerned primarily with the universal. It is always trying to get to God and to get the events of life into true relation to Him. So through Faith the humblest and most uneducated have access to an immeasurably vast world, a greater world by far than the world of physical science, the whole things of which the particular physical science are concerned with parts.

Faith, I repeat, is akin to genius. It is an instinct for the true heart of things, for the discovery of the riddle of the world. But that is not all. You say that science gives you the power to verify the intuitions of genius, that otherwise the most brilliant intuitions of its creative minds would be only guesses at truth. Is there anything like this in religion ? What is religion worth unless you can verify it ? Christianity would have died out ages ago if it had not been for the verifications of Christian experience. One of the inner secrets of its endurance is the fact that it is constantly verifying itself in the experience of those who believe in it. ' He that doeth the will shall know the truth of the doctrine.'

What emerges then when we look at the whole matter is this. In science we have as it were the apparatus of the mind focussed on a point, concentrated on details of the whole, whereas in faith the whole

mind and nature of man is front to front
with the whole besieging and enveloping
world. But it may finally be said, if this be
so why is there such a difference between
the progress of science and the progress of
religion? Why has the former, ever since
the true method was discovered, been so
steady in its discoveries and so victorious
in their verification, whereas religion has
had so confused and often so disastrous a
history? Why is it that to-day it is so
comparatively easy to attain scientific
certainty, whereas faith is often so des-
perately hard to attain? I take it that
it is just because of the great condition
of all faith, that it requires for its exercise
that you shall will the good, that you shall
recognise and obey the moral imperative
before you are in a position to solve through
faith the riddle of the world. You have
to obey your conscience in order to have the
very conditions of the problem before you.
The true reason why Christian faith is still
so hard for many to-day is that man, in

general, has never quite had the courage to make the wholly decisive experiment of casting himself absolutely upon God. We hesitate, as our fathers and their fathers hesitated, to stake life absolutely on the moral imperative. There has been one great exception. There was One once in history who had an unequalled intuition of God and an unclouded vision of moral truth. Not only so, but He made the final experiment—*experimentum crucis*. He died for His idea of God. He laid His life down. Ever since then history has echoed and rung with the verification : it is echoing and ringing still. There Jesus Christ has absolutely revealed the Father. 'No man knoweth the Father save the Son.' But for our comfort and joy He added to this the words, 'and he to whomsoever the Son willeth to reveal Him.'

LECTURE III

III

REVELATION

FROM among the questions which I have received since the address of last week was delivered, I see that the view of Nature to which expression has been given in these addresses has caused some difficulty, and before we go on to the main subject for to-day a few words of explanation are necessary. In the opening address I took Nature in the sense in which the ordinary Materialist regards it, or, more broadly, Nature as it appears in the ordinary scientific text-books, as the world manifested to us through the physical senses. Viewed in that narrower sense, Nature bears that sinister as well as beautiful aspect of which I have spoken. If you take it as a self-enclosed and complete whole, and further, if you endeavour to reduce the whole of the rest of human life to the Nature level, then you will find yourself constrained to look upon Nature in the way which I have indicated. But the moment you enlarge your views, the moment you allow that Nature exists for spiritual ends, you must begin to transform the conception of Nature with which you began. Then the Nature of Darwin and Huxley and Mill becomes the Nature of Wordsworth and Emerson. It is worth while to dwell for a little upon this point, for it is very important for our whole argument. I hope that now we are able to use the word Nature in a richer sense than we did in these opening hours of our common study. But to begin with, we used the term in its ordinary popular sense, or rather in the sense in which it is regarded in the scientific text-books, as a self-enclosed system of physical energy. With the introduction in last lecture of the thought of the moral and spiritual values which are being wrought out through

Nature, we reached a new point of view. From that standpoint Nature, instead of being a complete and self-enclosed system becomes simply the first act in a great drama, an act which is not separate and self-enclosed, but which is conditioned throughout in the poet's mind by what follows, and itself in turn influences the whole later development. We shall return to this, finally, in the closing lecture, where I hope to deal with the question of the supernatural in Nature. Meantime, it is enough to say that if Nature be but the first act of that great drama, of which history is the second act, and redemption the third, then we make the same kind of confusion when we try to interpret the vast whole in terms of Nature, as we should if we took the first act of *Hamlet* or *Lear*, and from the minute study of that by itself endeavoured to construe what the rest of the drama must be, drastically emending the existing texts of these later acts to suit our theory.

Why, we cannot fully understand any first act on a first reading of the drama. We have to work hard back upon it from the *dénouement*. The greater the poet and the more splendid his creation the more is this true. We launch out from the creeks and shallows of the opening acts to the wide, homeless deep, and voyage on through dawn and sunset and night, while we 'hear the mighty waters rolling evermore' till we have almost forgotten the harbour we left behind us in thinking of what lies ahead. But what work of creative human genius is like the vast creative work of God, which is lyric, drama and epic in one, the great poem in which you and I and all men and women have their part? Nature is only to be understood in the last resort as part of a whole. The real depth of meaning in that whole lies farther on than the first act, and in fact can only disclose itself when the climax is reached. The revealing things in Shakespeare are not in his first act at all.

'Revealing things': what are they? That is the subject before us to-day. What is Revelation ? We may give a preliminary answer to this question by going back for a little to the previous lecture. From the story of Lord Kelvin we saw that scientific genius displayed itself in a certain unerring instinct for the fact that was supremely relevant for the solution of the problem, the fact that was most charged with value and meaning. Is there not a general agreement that this instinct for what is relevant is always the first test of intellectual ability ?

Let me take a familiar illustration. Every student knows the difference at once between the man who in his books is all over the place, and the man who lays his finger on the points that really matter. The less gifted mind in every subject goes fumbling round the real point, turns down blind alleys, and wastes its energies in amassing irrelevancies, whereas the really able man, and most of all the man of genius, has a certain almost inevitable instinct for the thing that is most charged with meaning. I would again refer you to scientific and indeed to all kinds of biography of the heroes of knowledge, practical enterprise and religion.[1]

Now are there such supremely relevant facts in the great riddle of the world, facts which are more charged than others with the hidden meaning?

You must be careful before you admit this, for the moment you have done so you have in principle admitted the whole case for the existence of some kind

[1] I once put the question to a captain of modern industry: 'Supposing you had a big piece of work to put through, what is the first quality you would look for in the man you chose to do it.' He thought for a little, and then said, 'Perception.' This, he explained, as an instinct for the thing that needed most to be done. It may be of interest to record the rest of the conversation. 'What next?' 'Decision of character.' 'Rapidity or tenacity?' 'Rapidity.' 'What next?' '*Suaviter in modo*—the maximum of result with the minimum of friction.' 'What next?' 'I think that will do.'

of revelation. There is a loose way of
speech (I do not think it so fashionable
to-day as it used to be) of dismissing somewhat contemptuously the very idea of a
special revelation. 'Why,' says the critic,
'to me everything is revelation. It is
all alike instinct with God.' Carlyle said
that seventy years ago in 'Sartor,' and
many say it to-day as if it were a liberal-
minded novelty. Such talk is simply sand
in the teeth to any really earnest modern
thinker on the great problem. To-day it
takes the form usually of talk about the
divine immanence in all things. Of course
all religious thinking holds to the divine
immanence, but the whole question is as
to whether God is equally immanent in all
things, and whether, therefore, all things
are equally revelatory of their author.
Can any earnest and devout mind really
maintain this? Is God as much revealed,
for instance, in a cancer as in a healthy
organism. Is there as much of Him in
the Standard Oil Trust as in the Student

Christian Movement ? The supposition is monstrous. Not only religion but all idealistic philosophy is right up against this difficulty.[1] One of the best known ways of dealing with it is that which Mr. Bradley develops in *Appearance and Reality*. There is such a thing, he says, and in this he follows in effect a greater master of philosophy, as degrees of reality. The absolute is more fully present in some things than in others. In fact, however we put the matter, we must have some account of this clear objective difference in the facts of Nature and human life, not only if we are to be Theists, but if we are to have any really spiritual view of things at all. But if you admit that God is more present in some elements in the world whole than in others, you have practically admitted the existence of revelation and even of ' special revelation.'

What are some of the forms in which

[1] See G. F. Barbour's *Ethical Approach to Theism*. Blackwood.

the supreme Reality reveals itself to the spirit of man? Surely there is such a revelation in the amazing order of Nature which it has been the glory of science to have discovered. There is something extraordinarily like reason here in the constancy and orderliness of all things natural. Then, too, there is the wonderful beauty of much in the natural order which it is a sheer delight to think of, that beauty of Alp, and moorland and ocean, which they who have seen it feel in their souls to be akin somehow to the human things which are pure and lovely and honourable and great. All these, and much else in the natural world, are assuredly revealing things, which reassure us as to the source and end of all things.

But I do not wish to dwell on these things now. I wish to fix upon one luminous point in the great cosmic process, and that is the apparition within Nature of the human Soul. Let us imagine some observer looking down from above on the

G

great unfolding panorama of the history
of the world, seeing the whole sequence
of things from the fire mist onward, and
speculating as to the character of the
Being who was responsible for it all. I
think that as he watched the slow piling
of the strata, the apparition and evolution
of life in its lowest forms, the coming into
being, and the passing away again of
'the dragons of the prince' Dinosaurs,
Ichthyosaurs, and the rest, so uncouth,
so clumsy, and so brutal, as he realised
the vast amount of suffering in it all,
and yet at the same time the development of life, and the beauty of dawn and
night, of land and ocean, he might well
be perplexed as to the hidden Mind and
Purpose. Then out of it all there comes
at last into being the apparition of the
human Soul, and a new depth of reality
is revealed in the arena of Nature. Suppose an observer endowed with the power
of seeing the potential as well as the
actual in the soul of man, who could

divine all that would come to be in this
new world, all the divine beauty of conduct and emotion and thought, courage,
truth, and love, all that we mean by the
personal, would he not feel that here in
human personality there was a new and
revealing fact about the inner meaning
of those past æons, and the great system
of Nature about which he had been speculating? You know what it is to be
compelled to revise your judgment of a
man. You have been full of prejudice
about him, let us suppose, and you read
him in the light of those prejudices, till
he does something so undeniably great
and noble that you feel your whole former
judgment going to pieces. You have got
to think him all over again in the light
of this new and revealing fact. It is
just so with this apparition of personality.
You can say what you like about Nature,
that she is mother and destroyer, kind
and cruel, that she is full of beauty and
achievement, and yet of mystery and

failure and pain, but there stands out one
fact, clear and indisputable, there has
come out from her somehow the Soul,
and she has trained as well as begotten
the Soul. This fact is so momentous,
that in the light of it you have got
to think her all over again. You
have got to think out what the mighty
firmament means, what rain and dew
and snow mean in the light of the Soul,
and the new world of moral values contained in that word. The old conception
of Nature breaks up and is transformed :
the world is a greater world than you had
dreamed. We pass from the ' Nature '
of Huxley and Mill to the ' Nature ' of
Wordsworth and Emerson. For my part,
the whole of the beauty and order which
are in Nature become sacramental when
I look at them in the light of justice,
truth, and love. If nothing spiritual had
come out of this long travail, the beauty
of the world would grate upon me as
does the association of a beautiful face

with a false and malicious heart. I could
feel no joy in Nature if the soul of things
were indifferent or evil. I remember once,
on a first visit to Switzerland, spending
many memorable days in the high Alps.
For awhile the glory of the summits,
of peak and col and glacier was enough,
it was to me a new Apocalypse of Nature.
But there was something terrible and alien
in it too. It was an inhuman grandeur until
I had been able to get the whole work of
the great Alpine barrier in history before
me, to realise what the Alps had meant
as the rampart of Italian civilisation
against the barbarism of the North, and
as the cradle of liberty in later ages,
and, finally, as the creator of the great
rivers, the Danube, the Po, the Rhone
and the Rhine, with all that these have
meant for humanity and liberty. Not till
then could I wholeheartedly rejoice in
their splendour. I saw then that it was
eternally fitting that God should robe
these great archangels of his in stainless

and glittering raiment, and give them a formidable beauty like that of heaven.

So when you get all the beauty of Nature into the light of the great spiritual end, it becomes transfigured, and you can glory in sunset and dawn, and sun and moon and rain and dew, and every breath of wind becomes a word of God. Wordsworth has expressed that for us once for all in his 'Ode to Duty.'

> 'Stern Lawgiver! yet thou dost wear
>   The Godhead's most benignant grace;
> Nor know we anything so fair
>   As is the smile upon thy face:
> Flowers laugh before thee on their beds
> And fragrance in thy footing treads;
> Thou dost preserve the stars from wrong;
> And the most ancient heavens, through Thee, are
>   fresh and strong.'

So light begins to shine through Nature when the Soul appears. The drama has become vaster for you, just as when in reading Shakespeare you pass out of the opening scenes into the greater passages,

where the darkness gathers and the waters
deepen and the wind rises and the great
heavenly lights come out. Nature passes
into history. But with the growing
grandeur the tragedy remains, the old
shadows, pain and death, haunt you still
in new form, and a new shadow accom-
panies them—sin. So the thought arises,
' Is the soul, then, the last word of Revelation?' Is there no possibility that again
out of the deep, hidden world behind Nature
and the Soul, there will come something
into the world of time revealing yet a new
depth of things, and do for human history
and the world of human personality what
personality has done for Nature. It cannot
be 'something' if it is to meet the new
conditions established by personality. It
must be 'some one.' So we come inevitably upon 'the fact of Christ.' Do not mis-
understand me. Not for one moment would
I say that there is nothing of revelation
in history before you come to Christ. But
we must keep to the salient points, and

the central thing in history is the fact of
Christ.

Now, as I come to the heart of my subject I feel most acutely the old difficulty of
putting into adequate form the thing that
I most want to say.   My comfort is that in
such high things, 'a man's reach should
exceed his grasp.'

As one comes in sight of Christ, one
notes, first of all, that He is continuous
with history, exactly in the same way
as the Soul was apparently continuous
with Nature, so that one could hardly
tell when it actually began.   Just as in
science much of the best labour of last
generation has been expended in demonstrating the continuity between Nature
and the Soul, so in history has it been
with the demonstration of the continuity
between contemporary history and Christ.
Thus, any one who wishes to think of
Jesus Christ in a modern way must begin
with Him as a man.   I do not shrink from
this in the least.

Firmly as I believe in the divinity of
Jesus Christ, I cannot but recognise that
there have been immeasurable gains in
the preoccupation of modern thought with
the humanity of Jesus. ' It is not only
necessary,' said a well-known theologian,
' that we should know that God became
man, it is also necessary that we should
know what kind of a man He became.'
That is a pregnant saying. The history of
the early Christian centuries shows us a
certain preoccupation with the divine
element in Christ to the neglect of the
human. It is not too much to say that
theology gradually dehumanised Him, and
religion tried to deliver itself by bringing
in human mediators between men and
Him in the Virgin and the saints. After the
Reformation, again, the same danger re-
turned, and to many He became an official
Christ who discharged certain mediatorial
functions, or even a Christ who took the
place of the Father. Perhaps it had become
historically necessary that again in the

thoughts of men He should 'lay His glory
by, and make Himself of no reputation,
and take upon Him the form of a servant.'
Perhaps it may be reserved for the coming
age, the age in which you shall live your
life and do your work, to combine anew in
a nobler whole all that the scholarship of a
hundred years has done to make the Jesus
of history actual again with that most heart-
shaking and world-changing conviction of
the early ages, that here we have the
absolute and final manifestation of the
Eternal God, that these human lineaments
of the Man of Nazareth are the letters
and syllables of the Eternal Word. Then
the days the world will need sorely, the
great days of faith, will return, for 'Who
is he that overcometh the world, but he
that believeth that Jesus is the Son of
God ? '

I cannot give any advice to any one
here that lies nearer my own heart, that
springs more immediately out of my own
experience than this, that we owe it to

God, to ourselves, and to humanity, definitely to make up our mind about the Jesus of history. We have to sit down to those Gospel narratives, to study them, to dye our minds deep in them, to find out what kind of man He was, what He thought of God and of human life and duty, and to think and pray and act ourselves into that mind, so far as our conscience goes with Him, with the steady effort after fuller light. We have to deal with Him, to begin with, just as we would do with any great character of history. When we come to real difficulties as we shall in all probability do, places where our consciences do not at once recognise what He says as the highest, or places which the critical intellect fails to explain, we must not gloss them over, or content ourselves with superficial explanations. In such cases we must frankly admit them, and say, ' This is a real difficulty. I do not understand here, but I will go on and understand as much as I

can.' I believe that if you will loyally
and thoroughly make this investigation,
so that you shall have definitely fixed in
your own minds what the spirit and teaching of Jesus Christ were, so that you are
sure about that, so that, as it were, you
have a Christ conscience in you which will
enable you instinctively to know in some
measure what in your circumstances He
would think and do, then you will have
made a great step forward in the knowledge
of God.

The trouble with so many is that
they have so vague a knowledge of the
Jesus of history, that while they use
the name 'Christ' they might just as
well call Him by the name of the Virgin
Mary, or St. Francis, or even the Buddha.
Now that to-day is intellectually inexcus-
able, and morally dangerous in the extreme. It means simply that we will
not take the trouble to use the divine
revelation in the open Word of God,
and that as a consequence the Christ

Who should be a living personal reality is only a dimly luminous symbol of the good. The Jesus of history is one who can be known as a real man. I think that nearly all the living faith in Him which I possess to-day came to me along these lines, and I believe that this is the way out for you into the particular thing that God has to say to men and women of the coming generations.

But no doubt some will say at this point, 'You speak as if true knowledge about the Jesus of history can be attained, but can we really be sure that He ever lived?' That, as we know, is a question that is being discussed in certain circles to-day. I confess that it is one in which I find it difficult to take serious interest, except the kind of secondary interest which arises from the study of any eccentricity of thought or character. I do not wish to hurt any one's feelings, whether he be a student of literature or of religion, but the whole controversy

seems to me to be on the same plane as
the Bacon - Shakespeare craze. Life is
short, and the interest here is secondary
and pathological. When I find a scholar
who seriously maintains it, my interest
tends to pass from what he is saying, and
instead, I get interested in him. I want to
know what the intellectual motives are that
have led him to such conclusions. This
inquiry, I grant, has a very real interest
of its own, even although it is not primary.
The main inner cause of the whole theory
seems to me to be that modern thought
working on the historical material with
certain rooted preconceptions, has become
absolutely baffled by Jesus Christ, and im-
patiently gives up the problem. Sooner or
later this was inevitable, for these preconceptions have been deeply rooted in the
mind of the whole age which has been
so deeply concerned with the Jesus of
history. With some of these preconceptions I hope to deal ere I have finished
these addresses. But, at present, I can

only say that this contention that Jesus never lived seems to me essentially a *reductio ad absurdum* which ought to lead to a new examination of the premises.[1]

Now let us come to the picture of Jesus as we have it in the Gospels. This to me is the culminating point of revelation in history. It is the revelation of the solution of the riddle of the world. Let us come to the study of it as we would come to the study of the personality and teaching of any of the great founders of religion, who have each of them faced that riddle, and given us their solutions. The most important thing in every religious teacher is his idea of the supreme ruling world, his idea, above all, of God. Many of you have read Seeley's beautiful treatise, *Ecce Homo*, which after more than half a century is still a fresh and living book. There you will find that he says that the central secret of Jesus was His enthusiasm of humanity. That is a

[1] See for a full discussion of the controversy Loofs's book, ' *Who was Jesus Christ?* ' and, from a rationalist point of view, F. C. Conybeare's *The Historicity of Christ*.

fine saying, and up to a certain point true. But to my mind that is not the central secret of Jesus. It is very important in studying any character to get the central thought. Now the axial thought in Jesus on which all else turns, is that He was dominated and liberated by His enthusiasm for God.

This is the one central point from which alone you can understand His character. Face to face like all earnest spirits with the great riddle of the world, He is perfectly clear about the great hidden Source of all men and things. He knows It, He lives in It, He absolutely glories in It, and, alone among the sons of men, He is always proclaiming that the first and the radical thing that all men have to learn is unbounded confidence in Almighty God. It is true that to some extent He had been anticipated here in the Old Testament. There is no other book outside of the Bible in which such emphasis is put upon faith in God as in the Old Testament. It is the fundamental human virtue of the Old Covenant,[1] sometimes in its terminology appearing as Faith, sometimes as Belief, and sometimes as Trust. The writer of the Epistle to the Hebrews, in the famous eleventh chapter on Faith, has penetrated to the real soul of the religion and history of the Old Covenant. But if you will take any good concordance and compare the number of times in which, under these forms, the fundamental idea of faith is referred to in the New Testament as compared with the Old, I think that you may be as much surprised as I was to discover the new prominence given to faith in God. There are about thrice as many references in the New Testament as in the Old, and, when you remember that the Old Testament is thrice the length of the New, you get some very rough measure of the change that something or some one has effected in human thought, a change which becomes

[1] See Davidson's *Old Testament Theology* and Schultz's *Old Testament Theology*, on ' Faith.' Both volumes are published by T. and T. Clark.

the more remarkable when we realise the comparative poverty of the references in the literature of the contemporary Judaism in which practically all the New Testament writers were educated. Who effected this revolution in the scale of virtues? No one who reads the Gospels can be in any doubt about that. It was Jesus Christ alone. He came into an age which believed, with all Hebrew antiquity, that the world was fundamentally a moral order, in which the sin of man was punished by physical and outward tragedy. All the higher religious writings of the Old Testament, without exception, are penetrated by this conception, and it is carried on into Judaism. He came, He said, to bring in the Kingdom of God, and when you inquire what He meant by this Kingdom of God or Kingdom of Heaven you find that it was the overthrow of sin and the destruction of that tragic element in human experience which was its reflex, in other words, to naturalise heaven upon earth.

You may say that this linking up of sin with tragedy and death is an idea which modern thought has transcended. I would only point out in passing that, true or false, it is the conception that practically all the morally great imaginative writers of all ages, including our own, work with when they are labouring to interpret the substance of human life. You will find it stated in principle in the *Agamemnon* and *Oedipus* and in *Hamlet* and *Othello*, just as you find it more explicitly stated in the Hebrew prophets, that the world is a moral order, that the tragedy of human life and that racial and individual sin go together in organic union. The inner divorce from righteousness and God has its reflex in human woe. How else could God educate men?

Now Jesus came into this world to bring in the Kingdom of Heaven. He said that He had brought it, and He called upon men to actualise it by putting their whole confidence in God. He puts this faith in God

at the basis of everything else, as the one
thing supremely necessary for the soul of
man.   He says that He has come to bring
in the Kingdom of Heaven, that is to
say to bring Heaven to earth.   Read the
Gospels, and, in this connection, the Gospel
of St. Matthew above all, and you will see
that this is so.   He says that great faith
will produce great blessing, great actualisations of the kingdom.   That is the positive
assertion of the principle.   He puts the
principle also negatively.   He can do no
mighty works in Nazareth, actualisations of
the heavenly life, 'because of their unbelief.'
He states the same principle proportionally,
'According to your faith be it unto you.'
Finally, He reiterates several times the
great saying : ' If ye have faith as a grain
of mustard seed, ye shall say unto this
mountain, " Be thou taken up and cast
into the sea and it shall obey you." '   The
' mountain ' means, of course, any obstacle
to the coming of the Kingdom of Heaven.
When we examine in all its contexts what

this faith means, we find that it means
implicit confidence in the power and love
of God, and in His liberty to help men. He
is always teaching that, and His whole life
is one prolonged illustration of it. It is
instinct with faith in God as is no other
life in history. As one of the great Puritan
writers said, ' Jesus was the greatest and
best Believer that ever lived.' He has
wrought out His whole life so massively in
faith in God, that as you study Him you are
inevitably led out into the very presence
of God. The whole background becomes
luminous with the great Presence. He is
unintelligible without God. You cannot explain the Son without the Father. Abstract
altogether from His personality all that
theology has made of Him, if you will.
Let Him be to you simply the Man of
Nazareth, and none the less all that has
been said of Him above is true.

This Man has taken His human life and
made it luminous with God. One cannot
but marvel at the swiftness and security

of His sense of God.   You remember that
story of His going through the crowd with
Jairus, and how the fatal messengers met
Him and said, ' Thy daughter is dead, why
troublest thou the Master any further ? '
Every other human being in history, when
he heard that fatal word, death, would have
turned and gone back.   Jesus went on.
He went on though he knew that He was
risking all His reputation and message on
it.   That going on lets us see deep into the
very texture of His soul.   One stands in
awe before a man like that !   What a
sense of God He must have had, of the
reality and power and the love of God,
and of the liberty of that God to help
Him !   It is as unique as the deed that
is recorded to have followed on that
going on, and it is the whole theory of
the Gospel narratives that the one uniqueness explains the other, that He Himself
wrought His great deeds through His im-
movable and yet ' mountain-moving ' faith
in God.   He was continually staking His

life on God until it came to the supreme
experiment of all. There is no doubt
about it, Jesus died for His idea of God.
What produced the Crucifixion was the
final clash between the degraded Pharisee
conception of God and the conception
of the Son. He laid His life down on
God, and, according to the records, Nature
echoed and rang to the venture. He rose
again from the dead on the third day.
The thing that stands out, the more we
understand His character, is that God was
more real to Him than mere man, and all
the things of time were to Him as one day
they may be to you and me. That is the
'secret of Jesus,' not, as some have said,
the principle 'die to live,' nor, as others,
'the enthusiasm of humanity,' but the
immediate sense of the Living Father, pure
faith in God.

But, starting from this as the axial thing,
we find that out of it there springs unre-
served love for man. Love springs from
the faith, and reacts again upon it. Faith

and love are vitally and reciprocally
united. I believe that Christ's unbounded
love for men sprang out of this that they
were the likest beings to His Father that
He found in all the world.

In reading the lives of the saints of the
past, we are sometimes repelled by a strange
inhumanity to men. They do inhuman
things for the love of God, or they create
inhuman theologies with the intention of
'justifying the ways of God to men.'
They are capable of wonderful endurance
in witnessing to the eternal world, and of
absorption in divine things, but towards
men they are sometimes hard, and have
little sunshine and tenderness. Some of the
great saints of history have, for instance,
supported persecution. But how different
it is with Jesus Christ! He loved man as
no human being has loved him before
or since. It is the most reassuring fact
in history that He Who so loved men
had such unbounded confidence in God
Who ordained the great riddle of the

world ; that the Man who lived so close
to God found man so unutterably dear,
and the reason of it surely was that to
Him man was the likest being in all the
world to the Everlasting Father. The
whole story is suffused with this in-
expressible kindness, ' the astonishing
friendliness of Jesus,' as my old teacher,
Herrmann, used to call it.

Let us recall a few words of ' the Galilean
Spring'; 'My little girl, arise,' the story of
the Magdalene, the parable of the Lost
Son, ' Suffer little children to come unto
Me,' and then, at the last, out of the hour
of anguish, outrage, and gloom, ' Father,
forgive them for they know not what they
do.' What is there like it in history ?

And when we turn to the third great
characteristic, what other Gospel has dared
to put between faith and love this virtue
of hope ? Jesus had hope for everybody.
This was the magnet that drew the out-
casts and prodigals and Magdalenes to
Him. And he had not only hope for each,

He had hope for the world, for the victory of the Good. We may say of Him what was said of a great Christian of last generation :—'Hope burned and shone in him like a fiery pillar when it was quenched in all others.' We think to-day of hope as a happy accident of temperament or of fortune, but to Jesus and to the first disciples it was a great virtue, and therefore its opposite, pessimism, a sin. No modern writer on ethics would ever dream of so estimating hope. Hope to-day has a very different significance from what it had then. No doubt all of you are very familiar with Watts's famous picture of Hope. You recall the figure of that beautiful woman, seated on the sphere of the earth with blinded eyes, holding a shattered lyre and listening for the music of the one remaining string. Above her shines one solitary star. The picture is called Hope, but we might almost as well call it Despair. It is, at any rate, a very forlorn Hope. I have read several labori-

ous explanations of this picture, endeavour-
ing to explain and vindicate its title. I
respect their industry, but I cannot greatly
admire their insight. Is it not better to
say that this was Hope as the painter
conceived her? It was all that, under the
limitation of his age, one of the noblest
men and finest intelligences of the great
Victorian time could make of Hope. But
Hope of the New Testament type is a
very different thing. You can find a
better symbol of her in the Louvre, in a
famous work of pagan sculpture—the
Winged Victory of Samothrace. The Greek
called her Victory, but, shattered and
headless as she is, she is, to my mind, a
splendid symbol of Christian Hope, as she
stands there on the prow of the rushing
galley. Its speed is not enough for her.
Her great white wings are spread above
her, every fibre instinct with energy, and
she is in act to fleet away across the blue
waters to bring to some waiting city by
the Ægean Sea the news of Marathon or

Salamis. That is how the New Testament Hope strains forward. The whole book is astir and aglow with coming victory. Whence came that spirit ? It came from Jesus and Jesus alone. It sprang from His absolute faith in God, and if that faith in God were to be born again, even in our world of to-day, all the pessimism would lift and vanish like a mist and a dream, and the world would be young again by being born anew into the Eternal Life.

I think that you will agree with me that the greatest difficulty about this teaching is that to us to-day it seems too optimistic. The faith in God and in the soul of man, and in the great unknown future, seems too bold to be wholly reasonable in such a world as we are living in to-day. But for the moment let us try to imagine it true, let us take this figure as a true interpreter of the great riddle. Let us try to think of man as really worthy of love like this, and of God as deserving such unbounded confidence. Let us think

of the dark riddle as having so splendid
an answer hidden in its mystery. Let us
take Him, in a word, as the ultimate revelation. Does there not inevitably come
into our minds the thought of a hidden
world of beauty, goodness and life all
around us, into which we cannot come,
because of some strange palsy of brain
and soul, which compels us to think
false thoughts of weakness and despair?
Is it credible that such should be the
truth, that to-day with all our knowledge
we should be involved in such tragic
ignorance?

Let us digress a little. Some time ago
I was standing with a friend on a winter
morning in a high wood on the edge of
the spacious valley of the Tweed, by
the side of a newly opened prehistoric
grave. The workmen had opened it for
us, and we were about to examine the
brown earth within it that was all that
was left of what had once been a man.
We sifted the mould with our fingers,

picking out a stone axe-head and white fragments of bone. The thought came to us both of how different the world must have seemed to those poor savage men gathered there in presence of the great mystery of death, when that grave had last been open, from what it seemed to us that day. We thought of them living out their short and harassed life under 'the terrible conditions of prehistoric times,' in a land of marsh and fog and fever and incessant slaughter and premature decay, hardly able to conceive of anything better than the maintenance of the bare and stunted existence that they had won. Beneath us lay great spaces of fertile fields, a wide land of woodland and corn land and meadow and hill pasture; the smoke of a far-off colliery rose on the horizon; across the Tweed a train sped westward. Many a well-known homestead lay below. We knew the honest, wholesome life of daily industry and human loyalty, and reverent service of God that those home-

steads stood for, imperfect enough like
all things human still, but worthy of
all honour and affection, and with the
promise in it of greater things. But
all that wealth of Nature and humanity
lay all round those savage men hidden
in the earth, and hidden in the human
heart, and waiting for them to discover
and possess it all, when heart and brain
should have grown stronger and the social
league should have acquired a nobler
form. Have we any reason to suppose
that the same is not true of us to-day?
Is there not every probability that there is
a condition of knowledge and of life possible
for us all to-day, waiting for us in God
and in the soul of man, as much above
our present condition as ours is above
the condition of prehistoric mankind? Is
there not every probability in the light
of the past that the spiritual world which
is revealed in Jesus Christ is not an illusion, but the simple reality, so that our
supreme problem is to learn and to grow

in that revelation, and develop a common
life that shall enable us to attain it ?

Now, as we face this question as to how
we are to get the power to believe it and
to live it, we find ourselves necessitated
to examine the nature of the Christian
Gospel more closely. Is it simply teaching about the fundamental nature of
things, teaching that like all other human
teaching is limited and relative, touched
with error, and liable to be superseded
by fuller knowledge, or is it an absolute
and final revelation and redemption ?
Granting that Jesus Christ is a man, is
that all, or is there more that makes all
the difference in this vital matter of power
to redeem, regenerate, and save ? This is
the theme that lies before us in our closing
study.

LECTURE IV

IV

THE FINALITY AND ABSOLUTENESS OF
THE CHRISTIAN REVELATION

THE age which followed the death and
resurrection of Jesus Christ witnessed the
most wonderful outburst of moral and
spiritual energy that human history has
ever seen. This unsealing of new springs
of life and joy is the more remarkable
when we set it in its historical context.
Mommsen has summed up the condition of the Graeco-Roman world in a
memorable sentence : ' The world,' he
says on the closing page of his *History*,
' was growing old, and not even Caesar
could make it young again.' The best
index of the spiritual vitality of an age
is, perhaps, found in the temper of its
noblest teachers ; and beyond question the
soul of that classic age finds its best moral

expression in the Stoics. Lofty as is their teaching, it is all directed towards the schooling of men in endurance of the manifold evils of the time. There is no joy in it, no spontaneity or missionary power. The Stoic can call his own only the ground that he can cover with the sweep of his sword.

When we turn to the other great race, the prophet nation of the Hebrews, we find its spiritual representatives in Scribe and Pharisee, and in the unknown writers of the Jewish Apocalypses, which have been rediscovered, with such singular effect on our understanding of the New Testament, almost in our own day.

There is no doubt that the prevailing spirit of these writings is pessimistic. Their burden is that of Bernard of Morlaix in later ages :—

> ' The world is very evil,
>   The times are waxing late,
> Be sober and keep vigil,
>   The Judge is at the gate ! '

Like the Stoics, their purpose is to fortify the faithful, not to win the world for God.

Now, right out of this spiritually sad and dying age there springs the amazing outburst of life and gladness of early Christianity. What Caesar was unable to do, Christ has done. The Christian Church has lived spiritually on the New Testament ever since, because of its vitalising power. Yet the New Testament is only a fragment of an age written by 'a new race,' as they loved to call themselves, spiritually more alive than ours. The trumpets of the spring are sounding through all its pages. The narratives tell the story of the way in which the new life flamed over sea and land, kindling sad and weary men and women to joy and hope, abolishing enmities with love, lifting them out of sin into purity and peace, taking obscure lives and making them great. Not only is the soul of man quickened, but his brain is made alive after a new fashion. All through the book which is

the expression of this movement there
beats a storm of new ideas. The writers
are thinking all things over again in terms
of Christ and His salvation. Their writings
have for the student of their thought all
the interest of an explorer's chart drawn
by the camp fire at night, or as he voyages
down the great new unknown stream.
There is the thrill of discovery in them, of
discovery in the new name and purpose
of God.

> 'We were the first that ever burst
> Into that silent sea.'

Even disease and death go down before
that rush of life.

The contrast between these writings and
those of the Stoics is extraordinary. There
is in them an energy of hope and love,
and a confident faith in God which sends
them over land and sea to tell their good
news of God to all mankind, and fills
them with confident expectation of victory
over the whole world. The spirit of the
Stoic is one of noble endurance ; the spirit

of the Christian is one of world victory for Christ and His salvation. In the name of Jesus they face disease and death and sin, and bid them be gone before the power of the Prince of Life.

I remember some years ago spending a long summer's day alone among the ruins of Delphi. There, on a bare hillside, falling like a glacis from a precipitous wall of rock, lies a little quadrangle of ruin which is wellnigh all that remains of the religious centre of ancient Greece. There, around the inner sanctuary, each State of the Hellenes built its shrine to commemorate its victories. To-day the sacred way winds up the hill between the treasure-houses of Athens and Sparta, Thebes and Macedon. You can read, deeply incised in the stone, the very inscriptions which commemorate Marathon, Plataea, and the fatal day of Aegospotami, when the sun of Athens went down. All around you there is a wilderness of shattered marble lying in the sun, buried in deep grass and lovely wild flowers. Deep silence broods over all. There is not a sound save the cry of a hawk hanging in the blue, or the rustle of a lizard slipping like a green flame through the grass. All Greek history is there, the story of the most wonderful glory of the human intelligence that human history has ever known. But it is all dead and gone. The civilised world lives upon its achievements still, it is true. They quicken the artist's imagination, and inspire the wise man's thought. But Greece herself returns no more. The conditions which produced that wonderful outflowing of the intellect no man really knows. We may live on the thoughts of Plato and Aristotle, and imitate the works of Phidias, but we cannot produce minds like these. The fountains of creative inspiration are sealed, and the vanished splendour can never return.

Is it so with the great new birth of life of the New Testament time, which is supreme and alone in the history of the soul as Greece is in the history of the

mind ? Many think that that is so. But
that is not the teaching of the New Testament itself. The conviction which underlies and sustains it all is that here we have
the final and decisive opening of the
springs of eternal life for all mankind. By
the free gift of His own life in Jesus
Christ, by a decisive act of redemption,
and a final gift of the divine Spirit, God
has definitely answered that age-long and
world-wide prayer of the human race
which is the soul of all human religion.
That prayer is a prayer for life, and it is
surely no accident that the supreme possession in the Christianity of the New Testament is the indwelling of the Spirit of
God, that its central idea is eternal life,
and that its culminating fact is the resurrection. Henceforward it teaches throughout that man's supreme aim must be to
take home and to use the gift which, once
for all, God has freely given. If human
religion is, as scholars in the science of
religion tell us, a prayer for life, then

Christianity, as the New Testament shows, is the decisive gift of life. It is the supreme proof in history that God hears prayer. But if this be so, then, clearly, we have something more in Christianity than one religion among others; we have the one absolute religion among the many relative religions. We have the gift of life fully given that other religions are feeling after, and only experiencing in part. But, again, if this be so, then we must think of the spiritual glory that was early Christianity very differently from the way in which we think of 'the glory that was Greece.' That in its vanished splendour never can return. But, startling as it may seem, it is the teaching of the New Testament that there is nothing essential in the spiritual splendour of the days of early Christianity that may not return, and that is not meant to return. If the Christian Church to-day is not living on the ancient levels, it is not because God's gift of life has been withdrawn, it is because men will not appropriate and use the gift. The fountains of life in God have been opened once for all, and somewhere far above the low valley road along which humanity is toiling to-day with weary and bleeding feet, the fountains of life are still springing in the sun. Some day men will find them again, and human history will rise to a new plane. Some day the New Testament will become a new book, more interesting and more modern than the last book of science, or poetry, or international politics. For it is the faith of historic Christianity that it carries within it nothing less than the power of regeneration, that with the coming of Christ into the world there came also a divine energy of good which, when received by men, can transfigure them.

The great thinkers and poets of Greece explained and pictured the world as they knew it, the world of nature and the soul of man. But for the New Testament writers another and greater world had come dawning in upon nature and history,

the world of Christ and His Spirit, a world
of new spiritual forces capable of regene-
rating and transforming the human soul.
This world of life, they all believed, had
come to stay. It was destined in the end
of the day to triumph and to transfigure
humanity. It was, in fact, the *dénouement*
of all things, and in this creative evolution
of life they found the final solution of the
great riddle of the world. God had solved
it for them by the revelation which He had
given them in His Son. In Him the veil
which had, in all ages and lands, lain upon
the face of all peoples was taken away,
and it was now for men through faith to
take possession of Eternal Life.

Hitherto we have been developing the
broad Theistic view against the view of
Naturalism, but with this change of theme,
the disclosure of a new world of truth and
life in Jesus Christ, we find ourselves now
parting with some of those who have
borne company with us in our endeavour.
We have to develop our full statement of

Christianity against Humanitarianism, the view which makes Jesus only a man like other men, and Christianity one religion among the rest.

Now that is a great and difficult field, and it would of course be hopeless to enter into it in any detail within the limits of a lecture like this. I propose only to take a broad, general view of the matter, and leave it to yourselves to think and work out the consequences. There are here two different conceptions of Christianity. They differ in this above all, that the view held by both Catholic and Evangelical holds that God has done far more for men in Christ than the Humanitarian interpretation of Him allows.

It is not unfair in this connection to look at the history of Christianity. In the earliest centuries, and for centuries of modern history, there has been a Unitarian or Humanitarian view. It has produced noble characters, essentially Christian in spirit, who have often done far nobler

service to the cause of Christ than those who
professed a fuller view.   It has often, moreover, been a valuable critical leaven in the
Christian thought of an age, standing for
freedom and progress when the Church was
bigoted and narrow, and asleep to the Holy
Spirit of endless progress.   But the fact
remains that, taken as a whole, it has never
done the heavy lifting work of the Christian
Church, the inspiring and teaching of the
great masses of mankind, the winning of
the whole world for God.   It did not Chris-
tianise Europe, and to-day it is practically
negligible in the world mission.   Looking
away from individual heroes and saints
of Humanitarianism, and viewing it on the
whole as a historical phenomenon, it has
been something of a passenger in the great
ship of the Christian faith, while the men
who really drove it on through the great
waters were down in the engine-room or
up on the bridge.   To-day, you may think
it presents you with a simpler and easier
view than the other, but, tried by actual

results in changing and inspiring the lives of men, in the man its result is comparatively poor.

Now is there not something behind this ? What is it ? I believe it is this. Humanitarianism believes with Catholicism and Evangelicalism in the fatherhood of God and the brotherhood of man. But its God is a Father who seeks them only by the schooling of His providence and the inward movements of His Spirit in their hearts.

Now on the fuller view He comes right down into the heart of the world seeking His lost and rebellious children. There is a deep difference between these two thoughts of God. I wish to become a friend, let me say, of some great and famous man. I know how that friendship would cheer and broaden my whole life, and so I seek an introduction to him. If I am persistent I may get past his servants and into his presence, and if he is approachable I may get an interview with him. But an interview is not a friendship.

The more capable I am of the finer kind of
friendship the more I will feel that it is I,
and not he, who am carrying the burden
of it all, and I shall be constrained. The
very ticking of the clock will be a freezing
reminder of this. But it is a very different
story when he comes seeking me, and puts
up with all my neglect and rudeness, and
through it all keeps on seeking me, stands
at my door and knocks and waits. It is
a very different story when for me he bears
the extremity of anguish and shame, and,
though I forget even this, persists.

Such is the full Christian story of God.
He who believes it believes all that the
humanitarian believes, but he believes
more. He believes in a God Who takes
and keeps the most resolute and self-sacri-
ficing initiative, is not repelled by the sin
of man, but comes right through its burning flame, and, scorched and yet Almighty,
holds out His pierced hands of welcome
and salvation, and says, ' Come unto me.'
There is surely something here to shake

and move the very soul. If this is what has come to earth in Jesus Christ, then this is the greatest and best news of all. Better keep it even in an uncouth form, than lose it under the neatest and most easily believed formula of the study !

But is it really true ? I can well imagine a thoroughly candid and nobly disinterested mind which recognises the superior spiritual and imaginative force of what I have called the fuller view, which yet cannot accept it. I have had, in fact, the privilege of knowing some men like that to whom I looked up as by far my superiors in moral and spiritual things. But that humbling perception did not prevent me from believing that if they could get so far on a half Gospel, they would get far further upon a whole. So one is inevitably set on asking, What are the barriers which to-day seem insuperable to the modern mind when it finds itself face to face with the historical Christian view ? There are beyond all others, I think, two—the question of the super-

K

natural, or, as it is still called, the miraculous element in Christianity, and its claim to be the absolute and final religion. The one seems to clash with the scientific view of the uniformity of natural law, and the other with the modern conception of all things as in constant evolution. Minds which are constantly preoccupied with these ideas in scientific investigation refuse to cast them aside when they come to the study of the Christian Gospel.

Let us look into the difficulties and see if they are impenetrable. It is of course impossible to do more within our limits than look into them. I shall simply try to give the thoughts which have come to myself in trying to think the matter through.

But before we go further, let me go back for a little to the personality of Jesus. We saw in last lecture that He taught a doctrine of extraordinary elevation and purity, about faith in God and love to man and hope for the future, and that

His life was lived in singular conformity with His ideal. I do not suppose that almost any competent student of His life has any doubt that He was the greatest and best of all the sons of men. There is no need here to multiply testimonies to this by the great and the good. I will quote only that one which seems strangely little known and yet is, perhaps, one of the most striking of them all, the testimony of Kant 'who when his own name was indiscreetly placed by his admirer and future biographer in too near conjunction with that of Christ, . . . speaking of the two names, said, " The One is holy ; the other is that of a poor bungler, doing his best to interpret Him." ' [1]

But can we go beyond this, and say that Jesus was a sinless man ? That is a bold thing to say of any man. Yet there seems no doubt that His disciples believed Him to be without sin of any kind, for if they had

---

[1] John Cairns, *Unbelief in the Eighteenth Century*, Appendix, p. 205. See note at the close of this volume.

not done this, they could never have gone on to say that He was a heavenly Being, who was coming to judge the world. You only get the full meaning of this when you remember that many of them had lived in the closest daily intimacy with Him for three years, in which they must often have seen Him tried to the uttermost.

These men without exception tell us that they found no fault in Him, nor can they, in all His prayers with them and in all their friendships with Him, have ever found Him confessing and repenting His sin like every other human being who is morally sane. But we have more powerful evidence than even this. We have His own steady consciousness of being without sin, maintained from first to last. Now, we are all familiar enough with people who have extraordinarily little sense of sin either against God or man. There is nothing uncommon in this. But it is easily enough explained. There is no great problem in it. They have no high and exacting ideal. It is just so in matters of art. We are all familiar with the complacence with which many people regard their own poetry or sketches, for instance, and the pride with which they will show you their creations has something not only comic but pathetic. Why ? It is because their self-complacence shows that they have no real standard of beauty. Show them the real thing, and there will be an end of their satisfaction. So is it in matters of conduct. The moment we see what life ought to be, all morally sane men and women become convinced of shortcoming and sin. But let any one read the Sermon on the Mount and he will see how Jesus thought men ought to live. The only real fault to be found with it is that it is too high to be practicable. It convinces us all of sin. But here is the strange thing. It did not convince Christ of sin. It was with this standard in His soul that He steadfastly refused to confess sin, asserted for Himself spiritual lordship over all men and women and children, and said that the day was coming when all mankind, living and dead, would stand before His judgment seat.

It is this which makes Him so tremendous a problem to all who see in Him simply one man among others; one man, therefore, who, like all others, is subject to sin. Either He was on this point morally insane, or He was, what He said He was, without sin. But can we really think Him morally insane, this noble and gentle and mighty figure, 'Strong Son of God, immortal Love'? There remains only one alternative—namely, that here is One at last, who has broken the entail, and has Himself lived the life He enjoined on all others, of unbounded faith in God and unbounded love to men.

But if this be so, if in history there has appeared an absolutely unique Being, does not the whole question of miracle take on a new form? What is the difficulty?

Trace it to its roots, and you will find that it is this. Science presupposes always that Nature is a closed system, as it is called, *i.e.* that nothing happens in the world of sense phenomena that cannot be traced to causes and conditions in the same world of Nature, and that therefore the things which the Gospels ascribe to Jesus, the healing of the sick, the walking on the water, the raising of the dead, and finally, His own resurrection and ascension, are in glaring contradiction with this principle. We should not, it is said, for a moment believe such stories if told to-day of any human being. We should at once assume some mistake or some fraud. They would rightly be deemed incredible. Why, then, should we believe them of Him? The answer to me is clear. ' Just because He was Jesus, do we believe them.'

Here is, as we have seen, an absolutely unique Being. Be it noted, also, that His uniqueness lies just in those moral and spiritual things for which we believe that the whole world of Nature exists. We sought to prove, at an earlier part of our discussion, that the whole natural world found its final meaning and explanation in this, that it was meant to be the birth-place and training ground of souls, and that the supreme end of all that process was the bringing into life and full personality true sons and daughters of God, through all the tremendous schooling of pain and sorrow and death, as well as through love and life. We saw reason, in a word, to hold that the world was a moral order in which sin was penalised by tragedy and death, and in which goodness in the end of the day led to life.

Now, right in the heart of this system there appears One who has definitely broken the terrible inward entail of sin, who has in His own personality achieved the great end for which, according to our belief, Nature in her whole mighty frame exists, and has shown forth in radiant splendour of energy the inward

secret of faith, love, hope and life, so
that He is recognised as a true Son of
God at last in the world. What should
be our true intellectual attitude regarding the ways in which great Nature will
react to such an One? It seems to me
that the one supremely unwise thing to
do is to take up any dogmatic attitude of
denial. Here is an unique chance of
finding out something new about the
great mysterious world of Nature, her
secret intentions, the riches of her reserves
of power. What if she had all the time
been waiting for an *experimentum crucis*
like this to disclose her inmost soul?
This at least is certain. Inasmuch as
this life of His is an experiment that had
never been tried before or has never been
fully tried since, it is dull in the extreme
to assume that it can have no unique
result. What if, as Henry Drummond
once suggested, it should be as perfectly
normal for a sinless man to rise from the
dead, as it is for a sinful man to remain

in the grave ? What if perfect nearness to the Great Author and Sustainer of all should give a man power over all the tragic forces of Nature and time ? Would that not cast a flood of light on the whole long process of evolution ?

But, it is said, the axiom of the uniformity of natural law bars the way. With the utmost desire to meet all the fair claims of science, I cannot see that it is an axiom at all in the ordinary sense. It is a postulate, a working theory true within its limits, nothing more. I think that this is a view growingly held by the exponents of modern science themselves. It is impossible to discuss such a subject here in its fulness. I would only say that there seems to me one great fallacy running through much of modern writing on the subject. Science generally works with the idea that physical nature is a closed system. The text-books ask us to assume that nothing from above or below intervenes to modify or quicken natural processes. They are entirely within their rights in doing this. We all want to know for convenience and for teaching, how electricity works and how chemical forces work, and how, taken as a whole, Nature works, if left to themselves.[1]

But what they have no right to do, when they have finished their work, and mapped out their sphere and measured out their forces, is to take their postulates, granted for practical purposes, and turn them into axioms, to turn the 'let us suppose' with which they began, into an 'it is self-evident that,' and so forth.

I fear that I am growing too technical. Let us take an illustration of the point given recently by a well-known man of science. He supposes the case of a professor of chemistry working with his students in a laboratory. He is conducting an experiment which it will take a

---

[1] See for argument and illustration, Sir Oliver Lodge's *Life and Matter*.

whole night to carry out. So overnight he puts certain chemical substances in solution together into flasks, and says to his students that to-morrow [morning the chemical forces will certainly have produced certain results. So they will, if nature is left alone. He quite rightly ignores all disturbing forces of another kind for the purposes of his science. But all the same, it is always possible that certain enterprising and mischievous students, may break into the laboratory and mix his solutions, or that zealous charwomen[1] in the morning may dust his bottles and shake up the ingredients, and the actual result will work out very differently from what he expected. He ignores these considerations, and rightly ignores them. But they represent possible facts all the same.

Now, it appears to me that it is just so with Nature as a whole. Taken in abstrac-

---

[1] Lodge says that charwomen and students may be taken to represent Life and Mind respectively in the laboratory of physical nature.

tion from the greater spiritual world with which she is so intimately and strangely interlocked in man, the law of uniformity is true. But there is an interlocking none the less, and, given certain conditions, it may come into full play with results which, viewed from below, are miraculous, but from above are rational and spiritual and orderly.

What puzzles me not a little is to find that many who use this argument, that nature is a closed system, against miracles, are great champions of human freedom. But if I am really free, surely my will influences the movements of my body. It is quite impossible to hold this, and to hold that physical nature is a closed system. It is only possible to avoid this conclusion by denying that the volition or experience really causes the change. I confess that this 'psycho-physical parallelism' seems to me a hypothesis which, however widely spread it may be, is too glaringly in discord with facts to be anything but a temporary halting place of thought.

Yet further, I cannot escape from this conclusion when I think of other facts which I have known. There is a man who is living in the city from which I come who was a drunkard for many years. He was in prison one night, when Christ came to him in his cell. A few hours later, to use his own words to me, ' I cam oot o' twa prisons.' Since then he has lived a perfectly sober life, and the strange thing is that he has never, save once, even been tempted to drink. The desire has been ' sponged clean out of his mind.' There are many such cases. They are familiar to every mission worker. Now, here you have a change worked on the very physical tissues of that man's brain, which originated in the spiritual region. But on the ordinary physiology and pathology of the text-books there would have been no such intervention, for the physical processes are all that they, rightly enough for their own purposes, take account of. But life is larger than text-books, and reality mightier than abstract accounts of it.

Now apply these principles to the great deeds of Jesus. They are one and all, on this view, illustrations of the power of the spiritual over the physical, and the resurrection of Jesus is the crowning illustration of it all. Sometimes they have been compared to the bell which a crier rings to call attention to his message. The very grotesqueness of the figure is the best refutation of the theory. Imagine a heavenly bellman in this stupendous world of star and sun, of flowers and dew, of ' the moving waters at their priestlike task of pure ablution round earth's human shores '! No, they are part of the message. Jesus did not work them to show His power any more than a poet writes poems to prove that he can do it. He writes them, as has been truly said, because he cannot help it. So Christ wrought His works of wonder and love because of the energy of

faith that was in Him, and because of
the compassion of His love. Note that
practically every one of the great recorded
deeds of Jesus is like a revelation of a
higher and happier world. The dispelling
of disease of body and mind, the control
of the powers of nature that work tragedy
in human life, powers of famine and storm,
and finally, the control of death itself,
what are they but manifestations of the
life that shall be perfected in heaven, when
the long curse of man's history shall cul-
minate at last in reaching its home in that
infinite ocean of love and life which we call
—God? So they are, one and all, fragments
of heaven and 'intimations of immortality'
as the wild spring flowers that are already
appearing are prophecies and fragments of
the splendour of the high summer time.

If this view be true, how splendid is
the light these things cast back on all the
long course of nature and history! It
becomes all the way one long struggle
and discipline of spirit, which will come

to its true dominance in the Kingdom of God.

> ' And I—my harp would prelude woe—
> I cannot all command the strings;
> The glory of the sum of things
> Will flash along the chords and go.'

Is it really true science that bars the road to such a splendid illumination of nature and history as we get in Christ's victory over the powers of tragedy and death ? I cannot see that it is so. It appears to me that we get a truer interpretation of scientific method when we turn from the books of the men whose days of discovery are past, to the practice of the men who are actually finding out the wonderful new things. When I was a student I was taught by a justly famous teacher certain perfectly definite things about the properties of matter and energy which were expounded with his characteristic lucidity and decision. I know that if he were alive and teaching to-day I should find much of that teaching

L

radically different. What has caused the change ? It is, above all, I suppose, the advent of that strange little goblin, radium, which has suddenly appeared, and upset many of the orthodoxies of science. I have no doubt that, at first, many minds, held fast in the preconceptions that had dominated physics so long, refused to credit what they heard of it. But the *fact* of radium prevailed; the scientific mind recognised that concrete reality was richer than it had supposed, the old theories were scrapped and new theories formed to include the new fact. Now they are using the new fact as a new means of interrogating the physical universe. They are trying it on cancer and they are trying it on many things, happy if they can solve a few of the outstanding problems. That seems to me to be the true scientific temper. Now, if it be true science in physics, I fail to see why it should not be true science, when we come to the great problem of nature and spirit, to accept and rejoice in the fact of Christ. What if it be meant to reveal new deeps and possibilities in Nature herself? What if she were waiting for Him? Why should we allow preconceptions and prejudices to blind us to the fact that here, in this sinless One who has fulfilled the deep ethical purpose of things, we have an unique opportunity of testing and verifying the solution of the great riddle of the world? If we really understand His true greatness and spiritual beauty, we cannot surely find it hard to believe that He 'overcame the sharpness of death and opened the Kingdom of Heaven to all believers.'

And no man, who for himself and for others has ever looked straight into the eyes of death, can fail to find in that deathless story the very springs of courage and life, of belief in the ultimate goodness of Nature and of Almighty God, and in that heaven, of which our homes, now it may be broken for a little while, were but the parable and prophecy.

II

We have left but little time for the last
stadium of our inquiry. Yet it is, perhaps,
the most vitally important of all. Is this
Jesus Christ Who lived such a life, gave
such a revelation of the Father, died such
a death and rose again from the dead, is
He finally and truly understood when we
say that He is simply the greatest and best
of men, the summit spirit of humanity Who
has climbed to the heights and the dawn
and the vision of the great waters, and
calls to us, His brethren, to come up and
see the glory that He already sees rising
over this dark valley world?   If He is only
such, we may well thank God for Him and
for all like Him.   But is that all, or is
there more—more of wonder and hope and
arousal for the children of men?   Is there
that in Him speaking through all the lineaments of His character, as the thought
speaks through the Word, which forces
on   the   mind   the   amazing   conviction

that somehow God was in Him, that in
dealing with Him I am dealing with
Almighty God. That is the ancient question which is coming up in our day in a
new form in the question of the absolute-
ness and finality of the Christian revelation.
Is it the last word that we can say about
Jesus that He is a very noble teacher, who
is still far ahead of the world, but who one
day will no doubt be outgrown by humanity
as all the other great teachers have been
outgrown, or is He—Lord and Saviour,
God manifest in the flesh?

Let me illustrate the point by way of
contrast. History knows no chapters so
beautiful and noble as those which tell of
the coming of the great prophets and
founders of religions to the men of their
time. The story of Isaiah in Jerusalem,
of Socrates in Athens, of Zoroaster on the
uplands of Iran, of Gautama in the deer
park of Benares,—on all these immortal
stories there lies a light beyond the light of
time. They tell how great new thoughts

of the eternal things came to men through
the human medium of a noble personality,
how like magnets they drew to the new
teacher the flower of the nobler youth of
their time, who followed the master—

> 'Learned his great language, caught his clear
> accents,
> Made him their pattern to live and die.'

They one and all tell also of the great
fights of the spirit that followed the advent
of the new teacher. 'All things are at
odds,' said Emerson, 'when God lets a
new thinker loose upon this planet.'

Existing institutions, ancient customs,
old philosophies are always up in arms
when challenged, as they always are challenged, to the roots by a new religion.
There is a great fight, and often many
noble martyrdoms, and then, if humanity
receives the new message, it sinks deep and
moulds a new and nobler world which
seems to have come to stay. But the
destroying and creative forces of the spirit
work silently on, the new solution is found

to be imperfect, a new prophet rises within the area of the old religion with a new message, and the old battle is renewed. But this time, 'the rapiers are changed: Laertes wounds Hamlet, and Hamlet Laertes.' Those who were once the revolutionaries are now the conservatives, the teacher who was the liberator of his own generation becomes the gaoler of the generations which follow.[1] At last the forces of the free spirit break up the prison again, and the captive life escapes. We see that the message was relative to its own age, but insufficient for all: good for the clan and race, but not wide and deep enough for humanity. Is it to be so with Jesus Christ ? So say some to-day. They think that evolution forbids us to suppose it possible that at any part of an unfinished development in history there should appear an absolute manifestation of God, One who by virtue of what He is can at once be Saviour and Lord of all men. Is it indeed

[1] I am indebted for this thought to Principal Iverach.

so ? May the world some day produce a leader who will bring us nearer to God than Jesus can ? Is He God's message of Salvation to all mankind throughout all ages and lands ? If He is, how can we possibly know it ? Is it not enough to say that He is the highest that we know ? No, in the full Christian sense this seems to me not enough. If He is not the Lord of all men in all ages, I do not see how He can really be Lord for me, for if He can ever be superseded, I see no reason why He should not be superseded to-morrow or to-day. There is something vitally different in quality from the following of a man who may some day be superseded, and the following of One who in His own right is Lord, and in dealing with whom I feel that I am dealing with God. If He is only a man, why should He not be superseded to-morrow, let us say, by some spiritualistic revelation, or some new philosophy ?

But what are the grounds of my faith in Him as Saviour and Lord ? Like the first

Christians, we are for this thrown right back upon Himself. It is luminously clear that He always said that He was Saviour and Lord, and that He was the final manifestation of God. It is, for instance, certain historically that He said He was the Messiah. It is equally clear from the Old Testament and the Jewish literature that to their writers there was a sheer difference in kind between a prophet and the Messiah. To the Jew, the prophets were men who stood in the old dispensation and explained and developed its deeper truths, and in particular pointed on to a new and final dispensation of salvation, which should be brought in by the Messiah who was to complete the history of the world.[1] Jesus, certainly, consistently and repeatedly said that He was this Messiah, and therefore said that He completed the history of the world. He said of the great Baptist—the one man whom He seems to have admired—that He

[1] Herrmann's *Communion with God*. (Williams and Norgate.)

was greater than any prophet, that He was the forerunner of Himself : ' Verily I say unto you, among them that are born of women there hath not arisen a greater than John the Baptist. Nevertheless, I say unto you that he that is but little in the kingdom of God is greater than he.' In perfect consistency with this He made the tremendous prediction that all nations would one day stand before Him to be judged by Him. He said He was the final revelation. ' No man knoweth the Father save the Son, and he to whomsoever the Son willeth to reveal him.' And finally He enjoined on His disciples that they were to go forth and win all nations to His service, and said that, ' The gates of hell should never prevail' against His Church. These are but a few of the sayings of this kind that might be quoted to the same effect, and to my mind they are quite conclusive.

Now, we are left in presence of them with the alternatives of saying either that this was mad self-assertion, or that it was

absolutely true and therefore needed to
be said. We had at an earlier stage of
our argument to make a like decision to
that which is before us now. Were we,
or were we not, to assert the absolute
value of the soul over against nature. We
made the life or death spring of faith,
the judgment that committed us to a
spiritual view of the world. We have to
make a similar venture of faith when we
are face to face with this power of Jesus.
Either we have to say that He was a
mad self-deceiver, or that He was the Son
of God. Have we faith enough in what we
know of Him to follow Him further into
the unknown, to make this life or death
spring of faith once more, and trust Him
and risk everything on Him? We who
believe in Him again ' rest our whole
case on a simple judgment of value.'
Aut Deus, aut non bonus is the old Church
proverb, and in spiritual substance it is
true to-day. So we advance from nature
to God in history, and from God in history

to God in Christ. Through Christ there comes glimmering and shining the glory of God. We discern in Him God seeking us, coming through all our sin, bearing it, and putting it away, and drawing us into trustful and loving communion with Him.

It may be said, Why need we be so keen on showing that Jesus is more than a man like other men? What permanent religious interest is at stake in showing that in a unique sense God is in Him? I have already given one. It makes all the difference in the world to our life in God, when we know that He Himself has come seeking us, and is still maintaining that initiative, seeking and saving the lost. There is a nobler conception of God surely here than on the other interpretation.

But there is another difference of capital importance. The one vital necessity of religion is to be sure of God. For that secure knowledge of His will and character we need an absolute revelation. Now, if the revelation in Jesus be simply a partial and relative revelation, which we shall some day outgrow, it is clear that when we are really seeking to know the Eternal God, we must form our thought of Him in an eclectic way—let us say, from nature and history and Christ. The result will inevitably work out very differently from the God and Father of our Lord Jesus Christ. He is our Father,—yes, but we must modify this in view of some of the things in nature ; He is Love,—yes, but we cannot take that quite literally, for there are those strange things in history, and so on. The whole conception of God becomes troubled and darkened with doubt and fear. As a simple matter of experience, it is faith in the Eternal Son that above all sustains and renews faith in the Eternal Father. It is only when we take our stand firmly on the revelation in the Son, as the ultimate and absolute thing that is less perfectly expressed in nature and history, that the full forces of the Christian life can expand within us. There is a very great and vital interest of the soul involved therefore in this truth. What I want to know about this radiant life of kindness and faith is whether it is a mere episode in human history, or history's very heart and soul. I want to know whether it is an eddy or backwater in the giant stream of Time, or the great main current of it all. I do not believe that it is possible to live a rational and moral life in an irrational and unmoral world. Even so I do not believe it is possible to live a Christian life rationally except in a universe whose fundamental laws are Christian through and through, because its Source is Christ.

We can only live the Christian life when we are sure that the fundamental realities and powers are Christian, that Jesus revealed this very nature to the very core. Therefore it is no accident that, as. Mr. Glover has said in one of his books, the Christian life always becomes weakened when thought fails to give Him His own place.

Nothing else can sustain the spiritual energies of the world mission, the most daring and optimistic of all ventures of the faith.

I believe that it was a deep instinct for this truth that lay behind all the long conflict of early Christianity as to the divinity of our Lord. So long as we look at it, as Gibbon looked at it, as a controversy about the metaphysics of God, so long will it appear to us, as to him, a mere wearisome wrangle. But when we realise that it is Jesus whom they are talking about—this supreme manifestation of kindness, courtesy, pity, and strength—it becomes another thing altogether. These men, in a hard and brutal world of blood and steel and gold, are putting Love on the throne. They are making an affirmation not only about Christ but about the Universe. They are telling us what they believe about the very nature of things, that, in spite of all appearances, this is a Christ world. I do not think that we are necessarily committed to all their ways of putting it. We must distinguish between the substance and the form. But as to the vital truth of their contention, and as to the necessity of its substance, I am clear.

Let me sum up this part of our argument by a story. It is told of Thomas Carlyle that once, in Brittany, I think, he was passing a wayside crucifix. He stood for a little gazing at the bent thorn-crowned form. Then he said pityingly, ' Aye, poor fellow, your day 's up now ! ' Not a figure like this, but a figure like Frederick was to dominate the modern world. Time passed, and the great sorrow of his life came upon him. His wife died. Some one read to him, an old man in the chill and shadow of the approaching night, the familiar words, ' Let not your heart be troubled : ye believe in God, believe also in me. In my Father's house are many mansions : if it were not so I would have told you. I go to prepare a place for you.' Then Carlyle said, ' Aye, if you were God, you had a right to say that, but if you were only a man, what do you know any more than the rest of us?' There is much behind all that. If His day can ever be up, what did He really know of the abysmal Mystery that we can be assured of with the kind of faith that can overcome the world?

In the old days the controversy was as to the Divinity of Christ. To-day, it seems to me, the old question is up in a new form. It is as to the absolute Christlikeness of Almighty God. That this one Man whom humanity recognises as the ideal moral loveliness should be at the very core and soul of this stupendous world of nature and history, the most real Being in the Universe, who can wish for anything better than that? When we can realise it, everything becomes new. There is a new beauty in sun and star and flower.

> ' Heaven above is softer blue,
>   Earth around is sweeter green,
> Something lives in every hue
>   Christless eyes have never seen.'

' The most ancient heavens through Him are fresh and strong.'

M

III

We have nearly finished our inquiry into the Reasonableness of the Christian Faith. I have endeavoured to show, first, that the very conditions of man's personal life in the world of nature have set humanity in all ages and in all lands one fundamental and inevitable problem, the Riddle of the World. We have seen the close analogy between the genius which solves the particular problems of science, and the faith which solves the riddle of the world. We have seen a like analogy between the relevant facts, by seizing on which genius solves the problems of science, and the revealing facts which disclose the depths of the problem of the world. There is but one further step necessary to take to make the analogy complete and, I trust, to demonstrate that there is a deep, underlying unity beneath the processes of scientific reason and religious faith. The final step in the demonstration of a new fact or law is Verification. We assume the truth of the scientific intuition. If it be true, certain consequences will follow when we subject the intuition or hypothesis to experiment. If these consequences actually do follow, the intuition passes into accepted knowledge, and a new base of operations is ready for a new advance into the regions still unknown. Verification is perfected when we can prove the unity of the new fact or law with the whole of human knowledge, but that process is necessarily incomplete so long as human knowledge is incomplete. That a fact or law works out as true in experience is its primary verification.

Surely there is here again the closest analogy with the processes of religious faith. Human life has been so ordained by its Author that only he who will do His will shall fully know the truth of the doctrine. It is a law of the moral life that if a man will not act on his highest intuitions of Duty, he will lose those higher intuitions. They will gradually sink and waver, and at last

they will go out, and leave his soul in darkness. Even so is it with the spiritual intuition of the existence of God, the love-
liest and the greatest of them all. Tragic,
indeed, is his fate, who, with the urge of
all the upward progress of humanity behind
him, has fought his way on to that supreme
thing, that vision of the great Dawn, of
which all broken lights that have come
before are but the heralds, and then, having
seen the one thing coming that he was
meant to see, refuses to risk all upon it, and
adventure on the new journey through
lands as yet untravelled. For it is not
here wholly as it is in the world of nature.
In nature no man can evade the resistless
coming of the day. But in the world of
the spiritual life men and women can re-
trace their steps and travel back into the
night. They can relapse into the dream
of the World again. But they can also
verify that instinct which has come weav-
ing itself into their dreams, that the sun is
already up and nature awake and full of

light and song, and that a long, new day of energy and joy is before them. Men cannot solve that problem of certainty, with the statement of which this discussion opened, solely by means of the intellect. They must verify their intuitions by a decision and habit of the will. Faith, in fact, is an act of the whole nature, it is the whole man, intellect, affections, imagination, conscience, and will, seeking the whole truth, and throwing everything into the hazard. If we would increase our faith we must give the Eternal World the opportunity to verify itself in our experience. We must gamble with our lives on God Almighty. It is by such continual and increasing experiment and verification that the knowledge of God in Christ increases in the world, and that the truth about His Nature and Purpose is in process of demonstration. It has been truly said by a great scholar of the science of religion that the best definition of a saint is that he is one who makes it easier for other men and women to believe in God.

This is supremely true of Jesus Christ. By His life, death, and resurrection He has verified God, and has made it easier for all mankind to believe in Him. He founded the Christian Church that it might extend and develop that verification on to complete demonstration. Thus Christian men and women are they 'who through Jesus, believe in God,' and who are in the world that they may reveal Him. However far short the Church may have come in this supreme mission, it has not wholly failed. Through all the ages the succession of saints has been maintained who have carried on the verification of God. And though we are not saints we are born into a great tradition of verification of God, and we may transmit it greater and richer still because we have lived and died. Surely no greater trust can be given to the sons and daughters of men. To take this heritage of human life that is ours and to make it luminous with the glory of God, to begin each day with the confession, ' I believe in God the Father Almighty, Maker of Heaven and Earth,' and to go out into the world to prove its truth by faith and love and hope, and so to add our part to the growing demonstration of His nature and purpose, and the final solution of the riddle of the world, is surely a vocation great enough to make us glad that ever we were born.

EPILOGUE

V

EPILOGUE

THESE addresses were first delivered not long before the outbreak of the great war. Since then the great majority of the men who heard them have gone to the Front, and many of them must have fallen in battle. The war is a new event of immeasurable magnitude. It has compelled every thinking human being to raise the deepest questions, to examine, and, if need be, to revise his most fundamental convictions. It has antiquated, as is the way with all new facts, many time-honoured and conscientiously-held religious and ecclesiastical convictions. Is this true of the fundamental convictions of the Christian faith, which are the theme of this volume? Speaking for himself, the writer can but say that, far from shaking his own belief in these fundamental truths, the war has deepened it, and in particular the conviction that the Christian revelation gives in principle the only reasonable solution of that problem of evil which has always been the main difficulty of faith in God.

There is nothing intellectually new in the current problem of ' God and the War ' to any one who has really faced the facts of his own experience, and who knows anything of human history.   But what is new is the terrible emotional and imaginative realisation of the problem, of the power of sin, and of the illimitable pain and horror latent in human life.   It is one thing for a man to believe in God when sin and death seem far away, and another when sin has wrecked his life and his dearest are lying dead in the house.   The brute facts of the war have simply overwhelmed the faith of many, and submerged as well many a plausible sub-Christian philosophy, good enough for superficial living and summer

weather. Has the great tempest shaken
the pillars of the house of faith ? Can we
any longer believe in God ? Many are asking that question to-day, both in the camps
and at home. They are shaken to the very
heart by the ancient problem of evil—the
riddle of the world.

Yet however tragic for the time, and
for some, this doubt may be, we cannot
but be glad that fundamental questions
are up at last, and therefore that, if the
Christian Church knows how to deal with
these, the Divine Word of Revelation has
some chance of coming to its own again.
Before the war it may well be doubted if
outside certain limited circles there was
any real and deep knowledge of the sacred
writings among the vast majority of our
countrymen. Inquiries made from
various quarters into the mind of the
youth of our nation in the armies have revealed a startling ignorance as to religious
truth, which makes it very difficult to
believe that their minds can ever have

been brought into intelligent contact with the truths of revelation.   It may further be questioned if preaching generally was doing anything adequate in the way of teaching to supply the defect of education, to make intelligent human beings aware of the richness and grandeur of the sacred writings, and their relevance to the fundamental problems of every human life.   Perhaps the reason for the comparative failure of teaching and preaching alike lay in the fact that men and women generally were not facing these problems, had never felt their bare cutting edge, and therefore were not interested in their solution.   Many had a dim idea that the Bible was discredited by modern knowledge, and it had never been brought home to them as a whole that while criticism had shaken the traditional view of the Bible, it had brought to light new and wonderful aspects of the revelation contained in it, and so had made it a far more living book.

Whatever the causes may have been,

none who have any real first-hand knowledge of the mind of the younger generation
will maintain that most of them have had
anything but the dimmest knowledge of the
deeper meaning of the literature of Revelation. It may well be questioned if this
was not also true even of that fraction
brought up within the churches. Very
many were simply living on a vague
tradition, which was becoming vaguer
every year. Before the war much of
the apparent activity and movement of
organised Christianity was an expiring
momentum. In the great coal strike,
which seems so far off to-day, the miners
ceased their labours and there came a
moment when the entire industrial life of
the country was visibly dependent on the
stores of coal already accumulated at pit-
heads and railway centres. We were not
long in feeling the consequences of that.
The whole activity of the nation began to
flag and wane. Train services were cut
to the limit, food grew scarce and dear,

factories were shut down, and the streets became full of hungry and idle men. With ever-deepening apprehensions men watched the shrinking of the great ' bings ' of coal on which the whole life of the land depended. Every one felt that there was an end to that—that the end was drawing nearer. We all remember, too, the up-springing of new life when the miners went down into the mines again. Now we know that everything on sea and land depends on the toilers who are labouring deep in the hidden power-houses of the earth. Something like this is surely true of the sacred writings which contain the record of the Divine Revelation. The Church was to a large extent living on energy accumu-lated by past generations. We have all to get down into the ' unfathomable mines ' again, for the power that the new age demands. The analogy fails at one point. Every one in our industrial trouble could see what was wrong. Cause and effect were plain to the meanest intelligence. But in the spiritual life the malady was less easy to explain, and its causes were more complex. More was wrong with us all than ignorance of the Divine Word. But that this was one great lethal cause of the mischief may be made clear to any honest and careful inquirer. The simple truth is, that if we who are Christians conceived of Christianity as the great mass of the youth of our country conceive of it we should not be Christians. They are shut off from the springs of life to a startling extent by sheer ignorance and misunderstanding of the Divine Word. They do not know, and they never have known, the Christian solution of the riddle of the world. Their noble qualities are being wasted and thrown away wholesale through ignorance, which is largely due to the failure of the Christian Churches to realise and to make clear the faith by which they live.

Now the great riddle of the world has broken into their lives, and they have no answer to it. Is it surprising that religious

workers in the great camps tell us that while
more or less all the men in a dim way
believe in God, the one great problem with
thoughtful minds that outweighs all the
rest put together is the problem of ' God
and the War.'   How shall we deal with it ?
The first thing, surely, to make plain to
them is that the whole Bible from beginning to end records one prolonged grapple
with this question, from the opening pages
which tell how primitive thought conceived
that sin and death entered the world to the
closing pages which tell of the day when
' God shall dwell with men, and they shall
be His people, when He shall wipe every
tear from their eyes ; and death shall be no
more . . . and God shall say, " Behold
I make all things new ! " ' We have to
bring home to them that all the daring
and optimistic things in the Bible about
faith and love and hope were written
by men living under far darker conditions than we are now living in, that the
greatest prophecies and many of the

greatest Psalms, and all the New Testament were written by men whose country was like Belgium to-day, in the grasp of a brutal oppressor, men who were exiles and prisoners and martyrs, but who had found a solution of the problem of evil that made them stronger than the world which was seeking to destroy them.

What in brief is that solution ? We are far too apt to-day to say that all thought breaks down before the problem of evil, and that even Christianity has no solution. That is only true in a very qualified sense. That the solution is not complete, that there are unexplored regions in its dark recesses is, no doubt, true, but this is true of, perhaps, all the great problems of thought. None are completely solved. If we had an absolutely complete solution of the supreme problem its very completeness would make it suspect, for it would be incredible that beings morally so undeveloped as men yet are should be intellectually so competent as to have finally mastered the unknown.

Moreover, in the very nature of the case we shall never know the full answer to the riddle of the world until ' history's enormous spiral shall have wound itself to a point,' and we see the whole process complete in its final result ' under the form of Eternity.' But subject to this condition, we have in the Christian view of the world the only interpretation which is really in the field for any one who believes in the supreme worth of personality.

When all has been admitted as to remaining mystery, it remains true that Christianity has its own solution of the problem, by whose principles it must stand or fall. It would be strange if it had not, for, as has been said, it can be shown that the whole course of revelation, whether in the Old Testament or the New, has from beginning to end been intensely and persistently preoccupied with this very problem. The men who wrote the Bible have never been content to give that problem

up as insoluble. Such cowardice of thought
they would have taken as a betrayal of
the God in whom they believed, whose
character was apparently impugned by the
sinister appearance of the world which
they believed He had made. From beginning to end the Bible is the record of the
grapple of Faith, that is to say, of Reason
at its noblest, trying to solve the riddle of
the world. Such courage of soul and toil of
mind had their reward, for in the course of
the age-long grapple of faith every one of
the great truths of revelation was granted
to them, the discovery of each forming a new
stadium in the solution. It is impossible
here to go into the detail which is necessary
to show the truth of this statement. It
must, meantime, be taken for granted, and
the endeavour made briefly to state the
Christian solution of the problem of ' God
and the War.' Even this can only be
attempted in the briefest outline. To do it
in full would be to state the whole Christian
teaching, for the whole content of this is

included in its solution of the riddle of the world, of which ' God and the War ' is but a part.

It should also, further, be remembered that the solution contained in the Scriptures is not a cut-and-dried solution. It is given us in the form of great guiding principles. It is our duty to try to solve the riddle by applying these principles. But the application is left to ourselves, as is the way with all wise human teaching of adult minds. What follows is a brief sketch of an attempt to apply some of these fundamental truths. It may well be that particular deductions are mistaken or imperfect. They are offered simply as what commends itself to the writer and to many others who have already been at work upon the mystery, as a reasonable solution of the problem of God and the War.

Let us state then the problem that is harassing so many earnest minds to-day, ' How can God be good, if He has allowed, and if He does not stop the war?' It must be noted, to begin with, that if, pressed by this ancient difficulty, we deny moral character to God, we do not get rid of the problem. As we have seen in the earlier addresses, we are left with the riddle of the world upon our hands. How are we to account for an unmoral universe producing moral personalities? The only way of escape is to depress the value of personality, and to say that moral values are not absolute, that they are secondary products of an unmoral system.

If we cannot hold this, if we hold to faith in God, we are at once confronted with the question, If God be good can He be Almighty? The way out of the difficulty that is commending itself to many to-day is to deny His omnipotence. Now so long as this is a protest against vague and empty ideas of omnipotence it is all to the good. There is no religious value in ascribing a mere stark omnipotence to God that can make two and two five, or right, wrong.

This perverted conception is a mere idol, and the sooner it is broken up in the interests of reason and morality the better. But in their iconoclastic passion many to-day are, without thinking, going further. They are, in effect, asserting a dualistic view of things, in which God is opposed by a dark unmoral power as old as Himself, or, as Mr. Wells thinks,[1] older than Himself, with whom He is fighting, and with whom He calls us to fight, as Zeus might call mankind to help him against the older dynasty of the gods. He does not seem to see that this cuts the very nerve of hope. It has been truly said that the really interesting Being in his strange cosmogony is the Unknown Source of all things, out of whom his 'God' has come, the 'Veiled Power' which 'sits dark at the centre.' This Being, in the very nature of things, must have the last word as well as the first, and 'God' and 'humanity' must be but episodes in its life. It decreed the limit against which the finite

[1] *God—the Invisible King.*

God strives. It is perfectly clear that here we have no guarantee for the final victory of the good. The more we deny ultimate power and reality to God the more do we destroy that hope which is the soul of all successful struggle with evil. For if the older 'Veiled Being' saw 'God' come into existence, it will assuredly see Him go out.

This is the fatal sacrifice that we make whenever we endeavour to escape from the difficulty by thinking of God as limited by some power outside Himself, or, to use the popular phrase of to-day, by supposing Him to be 'a finite God.' Too much that is vital to man in his sovereign enterprise of overcoming the world is forfeited by such a solution, too much also that is essential to the life of worship and prayer. Religion, as a matter of history, has never been content with this solution. One of the greatest of all masters in the science of Religion, in the work which sums up a lifetime of labour on the faiths of mankind,[1] has said :

[1] Tiele, *Gifford Lectures*, ii. 93.

'It suffices for us to note the fact that man's religious consciousness has invariably caused the rejection of every system which limited the omnipotence of God in order that His holiness, righteousness, and love might be preserved intact.'

(1) Let us rather start with the idea of God, given as we believe by His revelation, and which is recorded in the sacred writings. Here He is revealed as the Universal Father, the Creator of all things, and the Almighty Sovereign of the world. Let us ask the question, Can He be really Almighty, if He cannot create. Surely of the two alternative conceptions, a God who can continually create new things of wonder and of beauty, and a God who cannot, the former is the greater thought.

(2) But the very fact of creation implies that the beings so created must have a nature and individuality of their own—an individuality which in man appears as Freedom, power to initiate new things, and liberty to choose. If men have not this

liberty then they are puppets and not men. All their devices and actions must be absolutely determined by God, and in effect He is the cause of everything that they do. They are simply forms of the Divine action, parts of God. Inevitably this view slips into Pantheism, and in this account of things there is no room for creation. If we are to be in earnest with the thought of creation, therefore, we must admit that it carries with it a true self-limitation on the part of God. The power to do this seems, therefore, to be involved in His very omnipotence.

But the freedom which He gives to His sons implies the power of going wrong. It is a gift which may be terribly abused. Is it unworthy of Him to bestow on men a gift that they may abuse, turning to tragedy what was meant for glory? We may ask why then are we to-day fighting for the freedom of the world? Why do we think it well worth while to lavish blood and treasure without stint to secure freedom for coming generations? We do not know that that liberty when won may not be grossly abused in the future as it has been in the past. We do know, also, that a wise and benevolent despotism often seems to produce a far better organised social life than our immature and untidy democracies have often been able to secure for their citizens. But we know this, also, that a free state can rise far higher than is possible to any despotism, and so we are willing to take all the risks of freedom, and to keep the road open to the highest.

Why should we think this the nobler course for us, and condemn it in Almighty God? May we not say that He knew that a free humanity could rise higher than was possible to any fatalistically determined humanity, and so for Himself and for us He took the risks of our freedom. A world built on these lines is a greater world than a world built on the lines of determinism. It has been truly said by Dr. Iverach, that it is a greater manifestation of divine power to make beings that can make themselves, than to make beings that cannot. For the former are men and the latter are puppets, and puppets after all are only things. But creation is not only a manifestation of God's power, it is a manifestation of His love. His love, like all love, is creative, desiring to create beings to whom it may communicate itself. It makes them sharers in its own creative powers, in human fatherhood and motherhood, in those gifts of genius which we call creative, and in those commoner gifts of daily life which give it its zest—the craftsman's joy in his labour, the business man's delight in his business, the mother's in her home, the Christian's in being a fellow-worker with God. It is as if the great Creator of all would keep back nothing of His own from us. He shows His greatness by making us creators too. Such is the view of things which seems involved in the teaching of Revelation about the creative

power and love of God and the freedom
of man. But a world built on these lines
has in it the possibility of tragedy, too.
Humanity may abuse its freedom, and its
very creative powers may be perverted into
causes of evil.

(3) It is the further Christian view that
in such a case, the reserved divine omnipotence comes into action, not by a violence
which would destroy man's freedom and
reduce him to the level of a thing, but by
the education of experience. We are under
a Moral Order. Men are educated by the
consequences of their actions. The men
and the races that will not live according
to reason and conscience and the soul
come up against ' the flaming walls of the
world.' This is one of the great persistent
ideas of Revelation, running all through
it from beginning to end. Like the ideas
of Creation and Freedom, it is one of its
master keys for the solution of the problem
of evil. The world is a Moral Order. Its
seeming anarchy is only apparent. Rightly

and deeply understood human experience is a vast system of education, in which by the tremendous reactions of the world upon them, men are being schooled in the ways of justice, mercy, and faith in God. Can we apply these mighty truths to the problem of God and the war, or does it fall outside the possibility of solution by such ancient and simple methods ? According to the Christian principles of God's education of man's freedom through the reaction of the moral order, the vast tragedy of the war would imply that mankind had somehow departed from the Divine order, and that they were now experiencing the consequences of that departure. Is that true to the facts? Let us hear what one of the ablest defenders [1] of our country's case in the great war has to say of the condition of European statesmanship on the eve of that war.

In a passage of extraordinary vividness

[1] *The Foreign Policy of Sir Edward Grey*, by Professor Gilbert Murray. Oxford, Clarendon Press.

he describes the condition of European international politics in the eight years before the war. He says that to him and those who think with him ' there is something sordid and even odious about the ordinary processes of foreign policy. There is a constant suspicion of intrigue, a constant assertion of " interests," a dangerous familiarity with thoughts of force or fraud, and a habit of using silken phrases as a cover for very brutal facts.' He contrasts it with home politics, where beneath all differences there is almost always a sense of the common good. ' But foreign politics,' he continues, ' are the relations between so many bands of outlaws.' He speaks of ' the curious mental atmosphere in which our international diplomats have to move. There is fear in the air, and it is fear that makes men lie.' He is careful to explain that these ' outlaws are not criminals.' They are by nature just as honest and honourable as other men. ' The real evil does not lie in the individuals, but in the condition of Europe.' He points out the extraordinary difficulty in which we are all put by this state of European society. 'Fraternity, public right and common sense; the problem is how to practise them or even remember them when we enter this marketplace of chaffering outlaws, each with a knife in his belt. It is not to be forgotten that we are outlaws too; that we too carry knives; that we happen also to be remarkably rich and worth robbing.' The power of all this lies in its truth. No one who has any real acquaintance with the history of international politics, not only for eight years past but for an indefinite period, can question it. Tried by any average standard of private morality it is a condition of sin. But if it be so, and if there be at the heart of the universe a perfectly righteous and loving Being, it is surely clear that sooner or later something like the war was bound to happen. Far from its being a difficulty of faith it is a confir-

o

mation of the Christian idea of God that
a condition of sin, such as is depicted in
the above quotation, is now working
out death. The life of the great nations
might have been a supremely noble
thing instead of this abominable 'outlaws' market.' The question who among
the nations was responsible for the 'outlaws' market' of the last eight years
is quite distinct from this. The great
majority of the readers of this volume are
no doubt clear as to where the main guilt
and responsibility lies, and in this the
writer wholly agrees with them. But the
entire international condition of Christen-
dom was morally diseased. The disease
has come to the surface in middle Europe
to-day in the truly infernal doctrine of
force as the last arbiter of right and wrong
as between nations, and like all diseases
it has to be met at the point where it has
broken forth, and definitely and unmis-
takeably overcome there. But our convictions as to this do not touch the main

point of the argument, that the condition
of international life before the war was
radically in conflict with the divine
intention and order, and that it has
brought us all up against the Nature of
Things. The League of Nations is an
endeavour to realise that eternal Nature
of Things.

(4) But it may be said that in this vast
tragedy the innocent suffer with the guilty.
If the guilty party alone suffered, it is
argued, it would be possible to believe in a
God of justice at least, but the states who
have suffered most have been those which
were comparatively innocent — peoples
like those of Poland and of Belgium, for
instance, whom nobody can rationally
accuse of responsibility either for the war
or for the ' outlaws' market ' which led to
the war. The Christian interpretation of
the problem brings forward here another
of its great central principles, its doctrine
of Vicarious Suffering. Judah faced this
very difficulty far away back in its history

when in captivity in Babylon. Granting
that its past history had not been guiltless,
granting the truth of all that the prophets
had said of its having departed from the
living God, yet that did not overcome the
perplexity or exhaust the problem. When
all was said, Judah and Israel had departed
less from God than Babylon had done, and
yet Babylon was triumphant and Judah
was in exile. Was it possible that God
could be almighty and just? We know
how the great unknown prophet of the
Captivity solved the problem, in the
wonderful passages regarding the 'suffering
servant' of the Lord. Judah, he boldly
says, is suffering for the sins of others, and
this is a principle of God's government of
the world. We know, too, how the New
Testament writers in their hour of spiritual
perplexity seized on this principle and
wrought it into the very warp and woof
of Christian thought, glorying in the Cross
of Christ, and in the law of Vicarious
Suffering as that noble law in human life

which has made possible the redemption of the whole world by the voluntary sacrifice of the Son of God.

Can we, like them, glory in the law of the innocent suffering for the guilty? Does it impeach or reveal the goodness and wisdom of Almighty God? Let us see what is involved in the thinking of those who maintain, as many to-day are maintaining, that the undoubted fact that in this world the innocent suffer for the guilty makes it impossible for modern men to believe in the goodness and justice of God.

What they desire is obviously a world such as primitive Hebrew thought believed in, a world in which right and wrong were strictly requited with individual reward and punishment, the world of thought whose break-up we see mirrored in the great book of Job. It is odd to find so many to-day who have never got beyond Eliphaz the Temanite in their thinking about fundamental things. If they could only see that law of individual requital in operation around them, then, they imply, they would believe in God. Let us examine their ideal more closely. In this ideal world, it seems clear, not only would it be impossible for the innocent to suffer for the guilty, but it would be impossible for any of us to gain anything by the virtues of others. Nobody finds fault with the great law by virtue of which all peoples enter into an ever-widening inheritance of honour and knowledge and power over nature, an inheritance which we all owe to the industry and sacrifice of our forefathers. What we do complain of is only that we suffer for their sins. But clearly both are simply aspects of the same great principle.

In this Eliphaz world of immediate individual requital, moreover, there never in fact could be any act of disinterested service, or of self-sacrifice and heroism. It is further clear that in it there could be no young children, no fatherhood or motherhood as we know them. It would be a hard, adult, legal world of individuals, each self-enclosed in his own *karma*, and able only to ' dree his own weird,' or work out his own salvation.

Who would care to live in such a world if he had the option to choose, instead, to live in our own infinitely nobler and richer world, the great human world that we know? With all its perplexities and sorrows, it is a world lit up with the lights of love stronger than death, and musical with children's voices and all that is meant by fatherhood and home, a world in which, as the Christian faith believes, it is possible for the Son of God Himself to lay His glory by and become obedient to the death of the Cross, submitting for love's sake to His own great law? In a world of mere requital there could have been no Christ and no Cross of Calvary. Which of the two alternative worlds is worthier of a God of Wisdom, Power, and Love?

(5) The fifth great principle of Revelation is found in the idea of the Kingdom of God, the faith that through everything, through nature, the tremendous discipline of history, the vicarious law, and the inward influence of the Divine Spirit, God is working out a purpose which in the end of the day will triumph, and which will justify all His ways with men. It is the apparent futility of so much human suffering that makes us doubt the love and power of God. If we could see any adequate end being wrought out by it all it would be quite another matter. Take the present war, for instance. Suppose it ended in the triumph of militarism and the return of a darker and sadder age, the strain upon faith would be great. But suppose it ends, as we have good reason to believe it will end, in a League of Nations, and the opening of a new epoch in human history, it will be far easier to believe in God, and in His government of the world. The vast and desolate battle zone of to-day will become

a holy place, where future generations will come to quicken their faith in Freedom and in the Future, and to dedicate themselves afresh to God and to humanity, where we may even trust that as at Gettysburg to-day North and South forget their enmities, the descendants of those who are to-day fighting to the death may commemorate the birth of a new order of democracy, international morality, association, and peace. Now it is an essential part of the Christian solution of this problem that through all human sin and sorrow the over-ruling God is working out something inconceivably great and beautiful, a form of universal human society as much above the world of to-day, as the finest form of human society is above the life of prehistoric man, something, indeed, indefinitely finer and greater, a Kingdom of God.

In an earlier part of this volume we saw how the whole course of Nature becomes transfigured in the light of the apparition of the human soul. This new thing makes it indefinitely easier to believe in God in Nature. So we shall never really understand History, including its darkest pages, until the Kingdom of God has come. It is an old proverb that ' fools and children should never see half-finished work.' So we may say is it with the riddle of the world. What we are looking at is half-finished work. The Cross of Christ itself was in this sense half-finished work. It only disclosed its meaning in the light of the Resurrection. So this great Cross of Humanity in the infinite wisdom and mercy of God can only be finally understood in the light of Humanity's coming resurrection.

(6) Finally, an essential part of the Christian solution of the problem of evil is found in its faith in Immortality.

It is quite clear from the story of the rise and growth of this belief in the literature of Revelation that it came out of the grapple of faith with the problem of evil.

Men were compelled to believe in immortality by virtue of their faith in God. There was no adequate solution of the riddle but along this road. So is it to-day with the problem of God and the War. Great as is the spiritual help which lies in the faith that the suffering and death of myriads of the present generation is working out untold good for humanity, we need the assurance also that their personalities are too sacred in the eye of God for Him to suffer them to pass into nothingness with the dissolution of the body. Nor is it possible for the human love that mourns them at home to win and hold to Him without that assurance, and the hope of reunion with them. But we are strangely weak to-day in the courage of faith which takes possession here of the full Christian faith. Pre-occupied and obsessed with this present life as we are, the life beyond the barrier, even to Christian men and women, seems too often ghostlike and unreal ; whereas to those on the other side we on this side seem, no doubt, literally as men that dream, wrapped in the great earth-dream.

On the Christian view of the world the whole vast process of Nature and of History, and of Redemption, is directed towards the making and the training of faithful souls who through death are born into that vaster life for which all things here are the preparation. No doubt, though we can only divine it as yet through faith, there is continuity between our life here and the life beyond the grave.

To a citizen of ancient Athens the life of his city was everything. It was a self-enclosed world, and when its sun went down it must have seemed like the close of a great and splendid tragedy. But to-day we know that the story of Athens was but an episode in an incomparably vaster history, and that in serving their city her great sons were serving the whole human race. All later history is different from what it would have been because of the

achievement of Athens in art and in
thought and in society. So the whole
story of the earth is no doubt part of a
vaster whole, and everything truly achieved
in its course, and every faithful human spirit,
and every sweet and noble relationship is
conserved and guided by the Universal
Father for the great life yet to be.

That through all the travail of nature,
and through all the tragedy and comedy of
human life, God is making a world of spirits
to whom one day He will fully communicate Himself, and who shall be united in
Him, is the final Christian solution of the
riddle of the world, and it contains within
that greater whole the true solution of the
problem of ' God and the War.'

NOTE TO PAGE 147

I am indebted to the Rev. W. A. Cox, St. John's College, Cambridge, for the context of this remarkable saying. Mr. Cox writes: 'The reference is to be found in Rosenkranz's *Kant*, vol. xi. p. 131.' Borowski, a Königsberg pastor, Kant's future biographer, had sent the philosopher, for correction, materials for an intended work, the publication of which during his lifetime Kant deprecates (Oct. 24, 1792). 'The parallels which have been drawn between the Christian morality and the philosophical morality sketched by me might be altered by a few words, so that instead of the names of those (*sc.* being set side by side), of whom the One is holy and the other that of a poor bungler trying to interpret His work, only those expressions which I have indicated would be used, because otherwise the conjunction might have something offensive in it for some.'

Printed in Great Britain by T. and A. CONSTABLE, Printers to His Majesty
at the Edinburgh University Press

CPSIA information can be obtained at www.ICGtesting.com
Printed in the USA
LVOW08*1816231013

358279LV00015B/975/P